ETHICS AS A BEHAVIORAL SCIENCE

By the Same Author

WHAT MAKES ACTS RIGHT?

PHILOSOPHY, AN INTRODUCTION

METAPHYSICS, AN INTRODUCTION

LOGIC FOR BEGINNERS

THE WORLD'S LIVING RELIGIONS

PHILOSOPHY OF THE BUDDHA

BHAGAVAD GITA: THE WISDOM OF KRISHNA

YOGA: UNION WITH THE ULTIMATE

YOGA FOR BUSINESS EXECUTIVES

TAO TEH KING by LAO TZU

THE HEART OF CONFUCIUS

POLARITY, DIALECTIC, AND ORGANICITY

DIRECTORY OF AMERICAN PHILOSOPHERS

Ethics as a Behavioral Science

By

ARCHIE J. BAHM

Professor of Philosophy
University of New Mexico
Albuquerque, New Mexico

CHARLES C THOMAS • PUBLISHER
Springfield • Illinois • U.S.A.

Published and Distributed Throughout the World by

CHARLES C THOMAS • PUBLISHER

Bannerstone House

301-327 East Lawrence Avenue, Springfield, Illinois, U.S.A.

©*1974, by* CHARLES C THOMAS • PUBLISHER

ISBN 0-398-03043-X (cloth binding)

ISBN 0-398-03044-8 (paper binding)

Library of Congress Catalog Card Number: 73 16166

*With THOMAS BOOKS careful attention is given to all details of
manufacturing and design. It is the Publisher's desire to present books that are
satisfactory as to their physical qualities and artistic possibilities and
appropriate for their particular use. THOMAS BOOKS will be true to those
laws of quality that assure a good name and good will.*

Library of Congress Cataloging in Publication Data

Bahm, Archie J
  Ethics as a behavioral science.

  1. Ethics. I. Title. [: 1. Behavioral sciences.
  2. Ethics. BJ37 B151e 1974]
BJ1012.B34   170   73-16166
ISBN 0-398-03043-X
ISBN 0-398-03044-8 (pbk.)

Printed in the United States of America

A-2

PREFACE

ETHICS AS A SCIENCE is an integral part of hominology, the science of the whole man, because ethics is man's concern for what he ought to do in order to attain the most of what is best in his life, and ethics as a science is man's effort to understand what is best and thus what is oughtness. That one ought to seek what is best should be obvious, and that one ought to avoid what is worst should be obvious. But what best and worst, better and worse, and even good and bad are somehow is not so obvious.

Part of the purpose of all other sciences—physical, biological, psychological, social and philosophical—and thus all other parts of hominology is to understand the nature of things so that we can know whether or not they may be good or bad for us. Each life exists interdependently with many other things, with things dealt with in each of the sciences, so that knowledge derived from all of them may help us to know what is best and to become more sure about what we ought to do.

Ethics is a distinct science since it has a distinct set of problems to work with (oughtness, obligation, duty, rights, rightness, wrongness, justice, conscience, choice, intention, responsibility). But it is not an independent science in the sense that its problems can be solved apart from solutions to problems confronting other sciences. Nor are other sciences independent of ethics. For the human purpose of each inquiry is to understand so that such understanding can be used to improve life.

The science with which ethics interdepends most intimately is axiology, the science of values. Since oughtness and ought-not-ness are defined in terms of goods and evils, understanding the nature of values is prior to understanding the nature of oughtness. Nothing is more central to hominology than axiology. Axiology is a distinct science because it has its own primary problems (goodness and

v

badness, means and ends or instrumental and intrinsic values, subjective and real values, potential and actual values). But it, too, interdepends with other sciences, especially epistemology (science of knowledge), metaphysics (science of existence), psychology (science of self) and aesthetics (science of beauty and fine art).

Knowledge of values is a kind of knowledge, so deficiencies in our understanding of the nature of knowledge affect our understanding of the knowledge of values. Do values exist? How do they exist? Does a self exist? How does it exist? How do values exist in and for a self? Lacking understanding of the nature of existence influences our understanding of how values exist. Inadequate comprehension of the nature of self diminishes our awareness of the locus of values, both those which are ends in themselves and those which are useful or means to ends. Failure to understand aesthetic experience as intuition of intrinsic value and beauty as projection of such value into objects reduces our ability to distinguish between the goodness of enjoyments, the goodness of symphonies, the goodness of machines and money, and the goodness of persons.

The entire scientific enterprise, whether focusing upon pure theory or upon practical technology—including ethics, axiology, epistemology, metaphysics, psychology and aesthetics—is needed for a full understanding of the whole man and of mankind as a whole. The effort to bring all such knowledge together so that the nature of the whole man can be depicted and apprehended is what is meant by hominology.

ACKNOWLEDGMENTS

Permission by publishers to republish the following items is hereby acknowledged with appreciation:

"Science is Not Value-Free," *Policy Sciences,* Vol. 2, No. 6, Dec., 1971, pp. 391-396. Published by Elsevier Publishing Company, Amsterdam.

"Some Principles for Choosing," *Philosophy Today,* Vol. IX, No. 1/4, Spring, 1965, pp. 52-60.

CONTENTS

ETHICS AS A BEHAVIORAL SCIENCE

PART I

INTRODUCTION

CHAPTER 1

OBSTACLES TO DEVELOPING ETHICS AS A SCIENCE

UNFAMILIARITY WITH the idea of ethics as a science often arouses fears, doubts and objections. Many of these are justified, for several kinds of obstacles hinder its development. Some of these have been collected and summarized under the following headings: misconceptions by scientists; popular misconceptions about science; popular misconceptions about ethics; failures by philosophers; and church-connected hindrances.

MISCONCEPTIONS BY SOME SCIENTISTS

What obstacles to dealing with problems in ethical theory by scientific methods result from misconceptions by scientists? Four kinds of mistaken conceptions will be examined: (1) Is science completely value free? (2) Is science capable of understanding values? (3) Do conclusions by scientists in some fields imply that ethics cannot be a science? (4) Is failure to develop earlier proof that ethics cannot become a science?

Is Science Completely Value Free?

Often it has been said that "science is, or ought to be, completely value free." Many scientists claim that "objectivity," the willingness to let the facts rather than preferences determine our conclusions, is essential to the scientific attitude. This claim is true. But the hasty, uncritical equating of "need for objectivity" and "being completely value free" must be rejected. Why?

Because science actually is saturated with values, as will be shown in what follows. Although only one example is enough to refute the "completely value free" doctrine, I choose the harder task of demonstrating a more thorough-going, more extreme, counter claim: "Not a single aspect of science is completely value free."

In order to do this, I select three major components of science, and show, with respect to each, why values (and value judgments) and obligations (and ought-judgments) inhere in working scientifically. Three such components pertaining to problems, attitude and method will be distinguished.

My usual method in demonstrating this claim consists in asking questions. My scientist friend gives his own answers. I cannot carry on a live discussion with each reader, obviously; but I can report the kinds of replies typically recurring in such discussions.

My first question is a general one: "Is science any good at all?" The reply is always, of course, a quick "Yes." Sometimes I receive a defensive enumeration of enormous benefits resulting from science, including greater understanding, better health, longer life and higher standards of living. Overlooked, usually, is the fact that such an answer provides a clue to the basic nature and purpose of science. "Why be scientific?" "Because being scientific produces good results."

Pushing this issue further, I ask: "Are *good* results enough? Or is science also *better*? Is it better to be scientific than not to be scientific?" Exceptions aside, where being scientific can produce good or better results, ought one not seek to be scientific? Test this question in another form: "Does it make any difference whether or not one is scientific?" If not, i.e. if it is a matter of indifference whether or not one is scientific, then no goods or oughts are involved. But if it does make a difference, i.e. where it is better to be than not to be scientific, then ought one not try to be scientific? The point pressed here is that such being good or being better is foundational to science. Such goodness or betterness is the very reason for its being in the first place. Hence, science continues to depend upon this value foundation even when it is forgotten. And the implicit "ought to be" scientific motivates one's behavior as a scientist, even when he remains unaware that it continues to be his basic ought.

Problems

If no values were involved in scientific problems, then it should make no difference whether or not they are ever solved. Yet, only a moment's reflection is needed to reveal the contrary. Let me put three questions:

1. "Should a scientist work at a problem that is not worth his while?" The normal answer is "No. A scientist ought not waste his time. He ought to work only at those problems which are worthwhile." Such an answer implies that every scientific problem is, or ought to be, a value problem. That is, a scientist ought to work at only those problems which have values in the sense that they are worth his while.

2. "Are all scientific problems equally worthwhile?" Or if some seem relatively trivial and others immensely important, ought not a scientist devote himself to the latter? Does not the relative seriousness of a problem constitute an obligation for a scientist to choose it? On the other hand, if a scientist regards an important problem unsolvable, then he feels no obligation to try. And, when the costs of trying to solve a problem appear to be greater than the benefits anticipated, then ought he not spend his time elsewhere? When the prospective evils outweigh the goods, does not the scientist have an obligation to refrain?

3. "When working on a worthwhile problem, how ought a scientist seek to solve it? Are some ways better than others?" If he is acquainted with alternatives, ought he not use the most efficient method? Is not a scientist constantly involved in value and ethical issues because, at every step on his way to solving each problem, he faces the question: "Which is the best way to proceed?"

Attitude

If there is an attitude essential to the nature of science, ought not every scientist have it? If he does not have it, ought he not acquire it? If he acquires it, ought he not maintain it, i.e. keep it in mind all the time he works as a scientist? Ought he not also urge his fellow scientists to acquire and retain it?

What is the scientific attitude? If a scientist does not know or is unsure, ought he not try to find out? My studies as a teacher of philosophy of science have led to the hypothesis that it involves at least three characteristics: curiosity, willingness to be "objective" and a willingness to "speculate" (i.e. attempt to formulate solutions even in the absence of assurance that they will work). If these are essential, then ought not every scientist have, or endeavor to have, all of them? The second deserves more attention, both because it is difficult to understand and because it is the source of the view that science ought to be value free.

What is "objectivity?" Is it something simple or something complex? Stated simply, it is the willingness to reach conclusions only on the basis of actual evidence and not on the basis of wishful thinking, prejudice, personal profit or fear. But complications appear when we study it thoroughly. My analysis reveals that it involves a willingness to follow curiosity and, as Socrates said, the argument wherever they may lead. It involves a willingness to be guided by both experience and reason, and, in the absence of first-hand evidence, the authority of competent fellow scientists. It involves a willingness to suspend judgment, or to remain uncertain, tentative, patient about one's problems until sufficient evidence warrants a conclusion. It involves being open-minded, or a willingness to be tolerant and unprejudiced concerning what the outcome will be. It involves a willingness to be neutral, impersonal and unselfish in whatever way is needed in order not to bias the results. Perhaps these distinguishable aspects amount to different ways of expressing the same idea. Yet an exploration of all of them may clarify, magnify and enrich the significance of the scientific attitude, and reveal both why it is important in science and why many find it difficult to understand, acquire and maintain. If all of these aspects are essential to it, then is not every scientist obligated to embody them within himself while he behaves scientifically?

Two more issues are crucial to understand what is meant by "objectivity." The first pertains to its relation to "subjectivity." Since subject and object are opposites, many quickly conclude that seeking to be objective involves avoiding being subjective. And part of the purpose of seeking to be objective is to avoid influence by subjective biases. However, "subject" and "object" involve each other. Strictly speaking, there can be no object without a subject, and no subject without an object. That is, no knowledge exists apart from knowers, and no science apart from scientists. Knowers, including scientists, are subjects. Why, then, conclude that seeking to be objective involves eliminating all trace of subjectivity? In fact, the scientific attitude is an attitude, and all attitudes are attitudes of subjects or persons. The willingness to be objective is a subjective willingness. Without this subjective attitude, objectivity would be impossible. So, ought not one who claims to be scientific keep in mind the necessarily subjective conditions of his efforts to be objective? Can one be objective in his understanding of science if he fails to recognize both subjective and objective factors as necessary?

The second crucial issue turns about the even less commonly revealed roles of wishful thinking, bias and prejudice in science. Has wishful thinking always led to bad results? Does bias always yield falsity? Is prejudice always vicious?

1. When wishful thinking produces bad results, it ought to be avoided. But if it helps produce good results, ought it not be permitted, or even encouraged? When one doubts whether a problem can be solved, if his wish to have it solved motivates him to efforts which do solve it, was not such wishing good?

2. When favoring one hypothesis over another leads to gathering evidence which would not otherwise become available, may not such favoritism be useful? Research directors sometimes employ scientists known to have conflicting biases, setting each against the other so that he will pursue evidence favoring his side more energetically, more persistently, more thoroughly. No matter which side wins, did not the directors rightly seek to exploit such biases?

3. Prejudice, or prejudgment, exists in scientists in many ways. Does not commitment to such views as "being scientific is better than not being scientific," "the scientific method is better than other methods," "a scientist ought to be willing to be objective," exemplify prejudices essential to science? Public adulation of science commonly ignores the fact that a scientist in his trial and error methods usually endures multitudes of errors or failures for each success. If, in the face of so many failures, a scientist cannot retain faith in the prejudice that it is the best method, he becomes a dropout. Various faiths, or assumptions, such as "the principle of the

uniformity of nature," "the world is completely understandable," "if it can't be measured, it doesn't exist," are neither self-evident nor empirically demonstrable; yet some scientists regard them as fundamental prejudices necessary to science. The claim that "science is, or ought to be, completely value free" itself exemplifies a prejudice. This one happens to be false; but, despite the resulting evils to be pointed out later, it does motivate some to demand rigor unlikely without it. Prejudice against prejudice is still prejudice. Thus prejudice is not, merely in itself, an evil. But prejudice which produces bad results is evil. Success in science depends not upon complete absence of prejudice, but upon the presence of beneficial prejudices.

Methods

If some methods are better than others, is not seeking the best method an obligation for scientists? Which is better? Without being exhaustive, I raise several typical questions about such methods.

1. If a first important step consists in clarification, definition and location of the boundaries of a problem, since otherwise efforts may be wasted exploring irrelevancies, is not a scientist faced with value problems, right from the beginning, in seeking a good definition and in avoiding evil wastes?

2. If, next, he must formulate a hypothesis, ought he not seek the best hypothesis rather than a poor, indifferent or even merely good one? If there are criteria for good hypotheses, such as clarity, definiteness, self-consistency, consistency with established theories, adequacy, simplicity, communicability and fruitfulness, then is not a scientist obligated to try to meet these criteria?

3. If verification requires testing, ought not a scientist conduct each test properly, carefully, precisely and well? If any test fails to be a good test by his standards, ought he not reject it and repeat it? When several tests are needed, ought he not try to decide in advance how many, so that fatigue, anxiety or haste will not be allowed to become deciding factors? If standards for minimum numbers or percentages of successes in trial and error situations have been established (as in testing pharmaceuticals on rats, dogs and monkeys before trying them on humans), does a scientist not have obliga-

tions to reach these standards before announcing success?

4. If an experiment is called for, is a scientist not obligated to design one which is clearly relevant, as adequate as possible and reliable? When methods for increasing the accuracy of experiments become available, is not a scientist obligated to use them? If some experiments are better in the sense of being more decisive or "crucial," ought not a scientist attempt such experiments whenever possible?

5. Involved in the foregoing are many subordinate duties, such as making observations, measurements and inferences, whether inductive, deductive or statistical. A scientist ought to seek good data, avoid erroneous observations, make readable reports and preserve his records. Surely his work is not good if his deductions are invalid, his measurements inaccurate, his inductions incomplete or if his statistical results vary more than permissible "probable error." If problems, hypotheses and verifications are not "scientific" unless communicable, does a scientist not have duties relative to communicability and actual communication?

6. If tools and equipment such as meters, telescopes, microscopes, transformers and computers are needed, ought not a scientist acquire them, the best of them, and then protect them from deterioration, theft or misuse? Ought he not seek to improve their accuracy, efficiency and endurance when possible?

7. When complicated problems require teamwork, does not the need for good research entail obligations to obtain highly qualified directors, well-trained personnel and enough men to do the job right? When faced with selecting and training men, ought not a manager seek persons with the best qualifications, including honesty, integrity, reliability, morale, adaptability, keenness of observation, inventiveness, skillfulness, good memory and good health? Ought he not also upgrade, retrain, remotivate and reward as needed? Ought he not seek adequate financing and prepare reliable and convincing reports for those who pay?

8. If pure research must be kept free from outside interference, ought not a scientist try to keep it pure? If research cannot occur without public or private corporation support, ought not scientists seek such support? If "pure science" remains merely speculative

until tested in practice, ought not a pure scientist demonstrate interest in, and when possible cooperate with, the efforts of applied scientists?

9. Whenever danger exists of unnecessarily duplicating efforts to solve problems, ought not scientists try to discover whether the experiments have been performed elsewhere? Ought not all scientists be concerned about rapid publication and wide distribution of results, and even of experiments under way, so as to avoid waste? When a scientist in one field discovers evidence of methods which he cannot use but which may be useful in other fields, ought he not inform others about it? If a new and better technique has been discovered in one field, ought not scientists in other fields investigate its workability or adaptability in their fields? When a newly confirmed discovery in one field implies need for revising assumptions or conclusions in another field, do not scientists in the one field have a duty to publicize it and scientists in the other field a duty to hasten to inform themselves about it?

I could go on endlessly asking similar questions. Must not the answer always be "Yes"? Is a scientist ever free from obligations? No, except perhaps when he finds time to relax from his duties, and even then it may be that he ought to relax, ought to relax long enough, and ought not to relax too long. Surely any scientist who stops to reflect, as we are doing, long enough to understand the nature of science will conclude that science is not, and ought not be, value free. Science is not value free. Science is value-full. Science is saturated with values. Surely there is no aspect of science which is totally value free and from which duties and obligations are completely absent.

Is Science Incapable of Understanding Values?

This question calls attention to conflicting claims by scientists. On the one hand, some say that science is unlimited in capacity. Although we do not yet and we may never actually know everything, there is nothing which in principle cannot be understood by science. Hence, science is capable of understanding values and obligations. We have not yet seriously occupied our minds with these problems; but when we do, we will be able to master them.

On the other hand, some claim that science deals only with fact, not with values. Such a claim usually presumes that facts and values differ in nature. If facts and values are entirely different and if science deals with facts whereas ethics deals with values, then science and ethics are entirely different due to the differences in what they deal with. But such a presumption overlooks contrary evidence obvious to anyone who stops to consider it:

1. There are facts about values: Is it not a fact that there are values? Is it not a fact that each value is what it is? Is it not a fact that there are different values and different kinds of values? Is it not a fact that each value has the kind of nature which it has? Is it not a fact that there are all of the values that there are? Is it not a fact that two values and two more values make four values? If a value ceases to be, is it not a fact that such a value has ceased to exist? If a value exists here and not there, is it not a fact that it exists here and not there? Do not all true statements about values involve facts? Is it not a fact about values that all false statements about values are in fact false? Can there be any values about which there are no facts? Can any value exist without there being the fact that it exists? Can any value exist without it being what it is, as like or different from other values and from all other things as it is, and without there being all of the facts about it that it is like or different in each of these ways?

Must not ethics, then, in dealing with values, deal with facts about values, and thereby also deal with facts? Is not the presumption that facts and values are so different in nature that there can be no facts about values mistaken? And is not the inference false that science and ethics are completely different because science does and ethics does not deal with facts? Furthermore, even if science were limited to facts only, how would this prevent science from dealing with facts about values?

2. There are values about some facts. Although most will admit that there are some facts which no one knows, which will never be known, or which no one cares to know, most will admit also that some known facts are interesting. In fact, each fact called to our attention becomes an object of our interest. (Ralph Barton Perry defines value as "any object of any interest." *General Theory of*

Value, p. 115.) Science is concerned only with those facts in which scientists are interested. Thus every scientist is involved in a value-centric predicament: he is interested in facts; his interest in them makes them values. He is interested in them either for their usefulness (i.e. in suggesting or testing some theory) or for their own sake; if for their own sake, then, as we shall show later, as ends in themselves or as intrinsic values; if for their usefulness, then as means to ends or as instrumental values. Thus, although not all facts necessarily have value, all those which interest scientists, or anyone for that matter, do have value as objects of such interest. Surely all will agree that some facts are more valuable than others, and even that the more we desire to know, remember or teach certain facts, the greater the value they thereby have for us. Hence, no fact of this sort can be entirely value free.

If so, then does not science, in dealing with facts, deal with them as valued facts, and in this sense as values as well as facts, or as value-facts? Hence, is not the presumption again demonstrated to be false; are not the assertion that "facts and values are entirely different" and the inference that "science and ethics are entirely unlike because what they deal with are entirely different" both false? Can science escape dealing with values when it values facts? Furthermore, even if ethics were limited to values only, how would this limitation prevent ethics from dealing with such valued facts?

Do Conclusions by Scientists in Some Fields Imply That Ethics Cannot Be a Science?

Although not all scientists in each field named need agree with the statements made below, some do; and their claims have been cited as evidence that problems in ethical theory cannot be treated scientifically. Hence, they serve as obstacles to such treatment.

1. Some physicists have said: "If it can't be measured, it doesn't exist. Values cannot be measured. Therefore values do not exist." If they do not exist, then of course there can be no science of values.

2. Some anthropologists, joined by historians and sociologists, proclaim cultural relativism. That is, the folkways, customs, mores, institutions and laws of one culture differ from those of another.

No universal mores have been discovered. Therefore, we have no basis for generalizing that some ethical principles are universal. Hence, there can be no science of ethics. Their moral advice: "When in Rome, do as the Romans do."

3. Some psychologists say that personality traits—including likes and dislikes, desires, hopes, fears and enjoyments, feelings of obligation, and conscience—are all products of stimulus-response conditioning. The study of stimulus-response conditioning is a task of physiological psychologists, physiologists, biologists, chemists and physicists. When these scientists do their work completely, the causes of desires, choices and feelings of obligation will all be explained. Feelings of obligation have no existence apart from or in addition to stimulus-response conditionings. Hence, there is no need for another separate science of ethics.

4. Some biologists, sociologists and economists, building upon the foregoing, add the following. Biologically, persons inherit instincts for survival and reproduction, including suckling the young, which makes possible survival of all animals, including man, without something additional called "ethics." Sociologically, persons are products of their culture which determines the structure of their minds, their ideas of good, bad, right, wrong and obligation through the need for group conformity, aided by language. Group-caused customs constitute morality; ethics as a science can do nothing except observe the geographical distribution of the prevalence of such customs. But this science is better called "demography." Economically, our existence is governed by supply and demand of goods and services, and the imputed utility of exchangeable things for increasing or decreasing our pleasures and pains. Although hunger, fear or advertising may produce feelings of obligation in persons to work, buy or sell, the instinctive profit motive and the laws of supply and demand suffice for a science of economics without depending upon any supposed science of ethics in any way. Such attitudes serve as additional obstacles to considering ethics as a science.

5. Some political scientists, legalists and specialists in jurisprudence say that no act can be held to be wrong unless it is a violation of a law. No laws; no wrongs. More laws, more law violations, and

hence more wrongs. Legislators decide what the laws are, and thereby they decide what is unethical. There is no need for a science of ethics which, if it existed, could merely report on the decisions of legislatures and, perhaps, modifications made by court decisions. Such views give no encouragement to regarding ethics as a science.

However, as we shall see below, other scientists in all of these fields make different claims. The foregoing assertions were based on superficial observations. As each of these sciences has advanced in complexity and in depth of insight, such conclusions were discovered to rest on hasty generalizations. Except where cultural lag still affects people in those sciences, most such simple-minded solutions have been superseded.

Is Failure to Develop Earlier Proof that Ethics Cannot Become a Science?

Students newly introduced to the various sciences find physics, chemistry, geology, biology and psychology with well-developed laboratory manuals giving directions for precise testing of established laws. But thus far no laboratory courses, manuals or precise law-testing exist for ethics. If it were possible to treat ethics as a science, would not such laws, courses, manuals and tests have been worked out long ago? Is not their absence sufficient evidence that there can be no science of ethics?

The superficial plausibility of this question may be seen by reading the history of the sciences. Each one encountered difficulties. Each had to overcome much greater difficulties than face ethical scientists today. We all know Galileo was arrested and tried for his scientific views. But surely no one today will be arrested because he regards ethics as a science.

Too many students forget that it took about 2000 years of development after Archimedes and Aristotle before the emergence of Newtonian physics.

> It took the physical sciences from about 1750 to 1850 to achieve a position whereby engineering could transform the physical world. . . . Then bio-medical sciences followed suit from about 1850 to 1950. . . . It is hoped that the century from 1950 to 2050 will be the period during which the social sciences will achieve a level of

respectability and acceptance that will pave the way for social engineering. . . .*

Would Hauser include ethics among the social sciences, giving it seventy-five more years to develop, or postpone its arrival until 2050 or 2150? Maybe you can, but I cannot wait until then.

If it took physics 2000 years to develop, and biology another 100 and sociology another 100, one could have said, as many did, that failure to develop was proof that physics, biology and sociology were not and could never become sciences. Ethics has been very tardy in its arrival. But does failure to develop at a certain time constitute proof that it cannot develop? Yet does not forgetting how much time was required for the arrival of existing sciences serve as an obstacle to arousing interest in developing ethics as a science?

POPULAR MISCONCEPTIONS ABOUT SCIENCE

Many persons believe that ethical problems cannot be dealt with scientifically because they have mistaken notions about science as well as about ethics. For example, when my beginning students were asked to assemble arguments for and against regarding ethics as a science, several misconceptions appeared. Some of these are similar and can be summarized together:

1. Science deals with universals, ethics with particulars. Science deals with uniformities, ethics with unique situations. Science deals with invariables, ethics with variables. Science deals with absolutes, ethics with what is relative. Science deals with unchanging nature, ethics deals with fickle men.

Common to all these views is a failure to distinguish between science and nature and between theory and practice. Each ethical situation is particular and unique. But also each physical situation —where two balls collide, a molecule forms or a seed sprouts—is particular and unique; each occurs only once and only one place and time. Science deals with universals because it deliberately abstracts relatively simple aspects from many similar situations. The remainder of each particular in such situations is ignored. Ethics as a science likewise must seek to abstract relatively simple aspects

---

*Philip M. Hauser, President of the American Sociological Association, quoted in *Science News*, 94:267, Sept. 14, 1968.

from many similar situations. It too must, as a science, ignore the remainder of each particular situation when formulating a general principle.

Each physical law is stated in such a way that it holds only under ideal (hypothetically fixed and isolated) conditions. It is so stated that all other variables are regarded as irrelevant. "The boiling point of water is 212° F." What this means is that if water is heated to 212° F under atmospheric pressure normally prevailing at sea level, it will boil if no other factors interfere. The boiling point of the same water atop a high mountain is different because the atmospheric pressure is less. But even at sea level, storms changing barometric pressure affect the boiling point of water. Hence, if water boils at 212° F under certain conditions, it can be expected to boil at 212° F again only if the conditions remain the same. Scientists expect their laws to hold, "other things being equal," i.e. only if and when all of the relevant conditions remain the same. Why, then, do people expect ethical laws to hold "regardless of circumstances"? Must not an ethicist, in order to be scientific, also state that the laws he discovers hold, "other things being equal," i.e. only if and when all of the relevant conditions remain the same?

Let us remember that the task of the scientist himself is to discover laws which he states as universals, other things being equal, and that the task of the engineer is to construct particular instruments to do particular jobs. The engineer needs to know both the universal laws and all of the many relevant variables before he can be sure that he can construct his particular instrument and that it will serve for his particular purpose. Likewise, the task of an ethical scientist is to discover laws, stated as universals, other things being equal. The task of the ethical engineer* is to help decide what ought to be done in a particular situation. In order to do this, he needs to know both all of the laws and the relevant variables, general (psychological, physiological, economic, educational, etc.) and specific (personal preferences, habits, manias, peculiarities of the setting,

---

*A term we fail to use partly because we have heretofor failed to develop a science of ethics, partly because each person wants to make his decisions for himself, and partly because specialists attached to institutions have specialized names, such as counselors, ministers, psychiatrists, personnel managers, administrators or policy scientists.

personality conflicts, what caused the problem to come up at the particular time, etc.), before he can advise with confidence. Ethical engineering, like chemical engineering, succeeds partly because the engineers develop skills, craftsmanship and artistic insight in comprehending particular situations and knowing which laws are and which are not relevant. Complicated ethical problems require specialists, such as marital counselors, child psychologists, gerontologists, credit managers and corporation "trouble shooters" who have become much more sensitive to which laws are operating and which other laws need to be considered also in deciding what ought to be done.

The ethical scientist, having discovered and formulated the laws, is as helpless when a practicing psychiatrist misdiagnoses a case as is a chemical scientist when a chemical engineer copies a wrong formula in preparing his compound. So long as popular misconceptions demands that an ethical scientist must solve all particular problems in advance by stating laws which hold regardless of circumstances, such misconception stands as a most serious obstacle to developing ethics as a science.

2. Science deals only with real things, i.e. things existing outside the mind or self, whereas ethics is concerned with choices, feelings of obligation, conscience, i.e. things existing inside the mind or self. Hence, what ethics is concerned with cannot be dealt with scientifically.

This misconception has two sides. First, mathematics, which some claim to be the most basic science, is concerned with numbers and with inferences or calculations about them. Numbers exist only in minds according to some mathematicians, and calculations about them exist only in minds according to all mathematicians. Using symbols to represent numbers—on paper or blackboards, in books, and now in business machines and computers—leads many naively to regard them as external objects. But a mind alone, inside a self, is all that is needed for mathematics. If mathematics is a science, then science is not limited to dealing with things existing outside the mind or self.

Secondly, although each person's choices, feelings and conscience are inside him, all of the other three or four billion people now

living are outside him. So an ethical scientist, in seeking to generalize about uniformities in ethical situations, has an almost endless
supply of real data. He may inquire, for example, whether a person
believes that he ought to choose living happily for one year or living
happily for twenty years, all other things being equal. In receiving
reports about such a question from ten, or ten million people, an
ethical scientist is dealing with things which are real, or outside his
mind or self, just as much as does an economist, physiologist or
physicist. That is, ethical scientists are not limited to investigating
their own minds, so even if science were limited to dealing with
what is outside of one's mind, such a limitation would not exclude
ethics from being a science.

*3. Science deals only with things about which scientists agree;
ethics deals with things about which people commonly disagree.
Therefore science does not deal with the things ethics deals with.
In short, scientists agree, ethicists disagree; hence ethicists cannot
be scientists.*

This misunderstanding also has two sides. First, although scientists in seeking truth seek to agree today as in the past, they continue to disagree about many important and very basic things. For
example, scientists do not even agree about what science is, what
constitutes the scientific method or what presuppositions are essential to science. Even within a single science, scientists often bitterly
debate basic issues. One of the sharpest issues occurring in my
philosophy of science course, to which I invited scientists from
several different fields to explain their conception of science as well
as of their own science, arose between two mathematicians. One
asserted that mathematics is not a science, because science is essentially inductive whereas mathematics begins with assumed postu-
lates and is entirely deductive. Another asserted that not only is
mathematics a science, it is the only science, and what makes all
other sciences scientific is their use of mathematics.

Secondly, ethicists also seek the truth and do seek to agree.
Although disagreements among ethicists should not prevent ethicists
from being scientific any more than disagreements among other
scientists prevent them from being scientific, the notion that
ethicists aim to disagree, or that they must disagree, is false. Granted

that when ethicists differ about their basic premises they will arrive at conflicting conclusions; but the same happens when other scientists disagree about basic premises. On the other hand, when they start with the same basic assumptions and observe the same three or four billion people with the same methods, what reason is there to conclude that they cannot agree about results? Of course, if some ethicists investigate rural and others urban, some ancient and others contemporary, some young and some old, some conditioned by one culture and some by others, then the results may be expected to differ. But, when different ethicists investigate the same people with the same methods and the same premises and with the same care, i.e. in such a way that all the conditions are observed to be the same (as is required in any sound repeatable experiment), why do some people presuppose that they must disagree?

Unfortunately people, expecting ethicists to disagree, look for such disagreements and overlook agreements. Disagreements are easy to find, partly because, as previously indicated, people expect ethicists to have ready solutions to particular, unique, complex problems rather than universals holding only when all other things are equal. Too often, when such universal principles are presented and accepted as self-evident, people brush them aside as insignificant or irrelevant. In doing so, they seem to insist on ignoring such agreements as do exist. Later I shall present some "principles for choosing." I have found no one yet who disagrees with any of them. Hence, it is obvious to me that the belief that ethicists cannot agree results from ignorance.

But the naive view that scientists do agree and that ethicists must disagree is another obstacle to be overcome before ethics can be widely accepted as a science.

4. Science is concerned with understanding, ethics with advising. The scientist seeks to know; the ethicist seeks rules for guidance. Science is descriptive, not prescriptive. Ethics is prescriptive, not descriptive. Hence, ethics cannot be a science.

This easy-to-understand distinction serves as a soothing platitude reinforcing beliefs based on the aforementioned confusion of theory and practice. Applied ethics does seek to help decide particular questions, just as applied science does aim to solve particular practical problems. But ethics as a science seeks first to understand. As a science merely, its task is finished when such understanding is achieved. Since ethical situations are complex,, and since new kinds of ethical situations emerge as megalopolitan, global and solar-space living develop, the work of ethics as a science may continue to expand as long as mankind embarks on new adventures. Even if, as appears to be the case with some long-established sciences, conclusions by ethical scientists come to be accepted as well established with respect to common and well-known problems, an open-minded, questioning and inquisitive attitude will continue to be needed by ethicists still trying to understand newer and still more complex kinds of problems.

Although pure science, whether physical or ethical, aims to understand, and its function as "pure" supposedly terminates when understanding is achieved, the purpose of all understanding, except what is enjoyed for its own sake, is to aid in solving problems, i.e. practical problems. In this sense, all of the sciences have a utilitarian aim, and the purpose of attaining reliable conclusions is that they can be used in practical situations where we are faced with the problem of what we ought to do. Later, when I have explored the distinction between "actual" and "conditioned" oughts, it will become clear that every scientific law may serve as a basis for many conditional oughts. For example, if water boils at 212° F, and if the situation calls for boiling water, then one ought to do what is needed to heat the water to 212° F. Thus the physical law about the boiling point of water becomes a crucial factor in a practical ethical decision. Such a law functions prescriptively in that situation.

Hence, the soothing platitude, "Science describes, ethics prescribes," misrepresents the actual situation. Ethics as a science seeks to understand the nature and kinds of prescriptions, obligations or oughts, but does not, merely as a science, seek to prescribe decisions for particular situations any more than physics does merely as a science.

POPULAR MISCONCEPTIONS ABOUT ETHICS

Unfortunately, confusion about the meanings of common terms is nowhere greater than in the field of ethics. Some of these confusions have become embedded in our language, are inherited as part of our culture, and thus help to shape our minds as we grow up. Although clarification must await detailed exploration in later chapters, a summary is needed here to demonstrate the magnitude of our problem. Doubtless misunderstandings here are greater obstacles than those relative to science. Their removal will make it easier to see how scientific methods are applicable; so long as they remain, such applicability will continue to seem impossible to many. These confusions contribute to contemporary demoralization, to cries such as "Down with the establishment," including established ethics. Although there are good reasons why we ought to seek to transcend the ethical, these reasons can hardly be apparent so long as such popular misunderstandings persist.

A first misunderstanding is that ethics is something simple. Although even a young child can learn that it is wrong to lie, even a life-long specialist in the field has difficulty keeping in mind all of the significant terms and areas needed for full understanding. "Value," "good," "right," "duty," "obligation," "oughtness," "conscience," "intention," "choice," "responsibility," "freedom," "virtue," "ideals," "standards," "codes," "conventions," "mores," "customs," "laws," "institutions," "etiquette," "conformity," "loyalty," "liberty," "sovereignty," "rights," justice," "purpose of life," "supreme value," etc., are terms loaded with controversy as well as confusion. Each has acquired many different meanings, and some of these have become so well established that their differences function as part of the vested interests of specialists in fields such as aesthetics, religion, anthropology, jurisprudence and economics.

A basic confusion persists in the failure to distinguish clearly between "good" and "right," and between axiology—the science of values—and ethics—the science of rightness, duty, oughtness or obligation. For, although there may be no rightness, etc., without goodness, there may be goodness without rightness. We can say that "This is a good apple" without implying that "This is a right apple." Goodness is something which exists prior to rightness, and without understanding the nature of goodness, it is impossible to understand fully the nature of rightness. Ethics as a science depends upon axiology. Axiology has problems of its own which can be dealt with, and solved, quite apart from problems in ethics. But problems in ethics, as a science and as everyday practice, can hardly be dealt with adequately without first settling the basic issues in axiology. Confusions existing in value theory constitute obstacles to success in ethics as a science. What are some of these?

1. Do the words "good" and "value" have the same meaning? Sometimes yes; sometimes no. When "theory of values" refers to theory about both goods and bads, "values" includes "bads." Yet, at other times, distinction is made between values and disvalues, or between positive and negative values. Do the words "bad" and "evil" have the same meaning? Sometimes yes; sometimes no. The "problem of evil" is complicated by the fact that some regard both "good" and "evil" as positive (exemplified in the Zoroastrian and Manichaean doctrines of two deities, a God of Good and a God of Evil) whereas others regards evil as merely the absence of good (exemplified in Neo-Platonism and Christian Science). Failure to define clearly the meanings of such basic terms as "value," "good," "bad" and "evil" prevents progress in axiology as well as in ethics.

2. Although "means" and "ends" are words which almost everybody understands, the problem of distinguishing them clearly and keeping the distinction in mind is both one of the most difficult and one of the most necessary conditions of clear thinking about values and ethics. Technically, means are called "instrumental values" and ends "intrinsic values." Intrinsic values are values which are ends in themselves, thus requiring no other ends in order to be value. Instrumental values are means to ends, thus both serving to cause or maintain ends in themselves, and having their own value, as instrumental, dependent for its existence as value upon the ends served. How ends depend upon means to cause them and how means depend upon ends for their value often puzzles beginners. The issue is complicated further by the fact that the same thing, person or event may, and often does, embody both. The pleasing flavor of a delicious chocolate, although enjoyed as an end in itself, arouses in me desire for another, thereby serving as a means to an end. Although being muddled about the means-end distinction is serious enough merely in axiology, it becomes crucial in ethics where failure to differentiate between conditional

and actual oughts yields befuddlement and helplessness.

3. Focusing attention on intrinsic value, we find another batch of perplexing questions and another whole nest of pestiferous controversies. Are intrinsic values static or changing, temporal or eternal, temporary or indestructible? Is there only one intrinsic value in the universe, such as God or Brahman, or many, such as many persons? Is each person only one intrinsic value or many? *Is* a person an intrinsic value or does he merely *have* intrinsic value? Is there only one kind of intrinsic value or are there many different kinds? Do intrinsic values exist only inside persons, only outside persons or both? What is the nature of a person that he should be or have value? What is the nature of things if they are or have intrinsic value? Thus an investigator finds himself involved in hosts of metaphysical problems. How can he understand the nature of intrinsic value until he resolves all such metaphysical problems?

Before he solves these, he finds himself faced with the question of how values are known? Are intrinsic values knowable? Some say yes; some say no. So he encounters many intricate epistemological problems. And epistemologists commonly regard knowledge of values as the most difficult kind of knowledge to deal with. Experts usually conclude that, in order to be known, intrinsic values must be intuited. But since the term "intuition" has been so much abused and has gathered a backlog of disrepute, they hesitate to use it; and when they do use it, they often fail to communicate because the disreputable meanings are better known. Technical references to intuited values as "indefinable" have crept into popular literature, contributing further to general obfuscation.

Intuition of intrinsic value is essentially an aesthetic experience. That is, when an experience is enjoyed as an end in itself and as lacking nothing in order to be complete, it is properly spoken of as aesthetic. Hence, a knowing ethicist must be an aesthetician, at least so far as appreciation of intrinsic values is concerned. But aesthetics, although a science in itself and one also depending upon axiology, has its own plethora of issues to resolve; and its association with philosophy of the fine are involves it in multitudes of complexities which had better be avoided if one expects to spend much time making progress toward ethics as a science. Yet, since, for example, experiences of beauty and experiences projecting ethical ideals have much in common, an ethicist who ignores aesthetics endangers his chances of achieveing fully satisfactory views. (Experiences of beauty involving a subjective enjoyment of intrinsic value occur with the beauty appearing as if outside the person and in an external painting, sunset or attractive smile. Ethical ideals are also subjective and also appear as if the goals sought are values appearing as if existing outside the present and in the future.) Furthermore, popular awareness that artists often gain a reputation for immorality because uninhibited by local mores leads some to believe, mistakenly, that ethics and aesthetics are incompatible. Although such views may seem relatively trivial, they contribute their bit to prevailing doubts that ethical problems can ever be solved scientifically if they must depend upon the scientific solution of aesthetic problems.

Next, let us recall that, when considering the intrinsic value of a life as a whole, we plunge into the heart of philosophy of religion. Aesthetics, ethics and philosophy of religion, all standing on axiological bases, overlap and supplement each other. Not only do enjoyments of natural and artistic beauties enhance the value of one's life, but an artistically lived life, enjoyed as an end in itself, has aesthetic value and may be both understood and appreciated better by studying aesthetics as a science. The purpose or goal of life, regardless of whether attainment is expected only after death or enjoyed day by day, can be enjoyed as an end in itself only aesthetically. The goal of religion is aesthetic enjoyment; the way to an unattained goal involves moral endeavor. Thus one can hardly understand religion without understanding both ethics and aesthetics. Furthermore, if the goal of life is one's highest value, then the obligation to attain it becomes greater than all other oughts. The point being emphasized here is that even axiology, as well as ethics, entails issues in philosophy of religion as well as those in metaphysics, epistemology and aesthetics. Hence, the need for competent handling of such issues is needed for success in developing ethics as a science. Such competence can be achieved, but since the study and teaching of philosophy of religion is cluttered with multitudes of issues inherent in the history of sectarianism, the need for wading through volumes of sectarian bias, discovering the general nature of religion after sifting out the peculiarities of all of them, and rising above them with a clearer vision, serves as a hurdle, or rather a series of hurdles, which some would-be ethicists never manager to get over.

One final obstacle to clarity regarding intrinsic value is the fact that economists have adopted a misuse of the term when saying that gold coins have intrinsic value whereas paper money does not. What they mean is that the metal can be used for other purposes, i.e. it has many different potential instrumental values, whereas the paper out of which paper money is made does not. To my claim of "misuse," economists will reply that people can use their words in any way they choose to, and since economists have adopted this usage as standard, no one else is justified in being critical. But the problem remains. When a student of economics, the science of wealth or of economic values consults an economist's lexicon, he finds that the word "intrinsic value" means something quite different from what it does in axiology. With a mind tuned to "utility," "exchange value," "price" and "credit"—values based upon, yet quite removed from, intuited enjoyments as ends in themselves—he usually experiences some difficulty in adjusting his mind to the language needed in axiology. Thus, although studies in economics (and in anthropology, sociology and political science) may provide support for the development of ethics as a science, on the other hand, insistence upon maintaining linguistic practices established in the absence of axiology and ethics as sciences may serve as obstacles to such development.

4. Another distinction necessary to understanding values is so troublesome that even technical experts would like to avoid it and tend to postpone considering it as long as possible. This is the distinction between potential and actual values, including both potential and actual instrumental and potential and actual intrinsic values. Even merely as a metaphiysical problem, understanding the difference between and the interdependence of potentiality and actuality, or of potency and act, is notorious for its difficulty. And those seeking information from sources which do not take account

of newer dynamic solutions to potential-actual problems may remain trapped in and paralyzed by paradoxes inherent in static metaphysical systems. Compounding axiological with metaphysical difficulties doubtless causes some to abandon their quest. But since understanding this distinction is prerequisite to comprehending one of the most basic distinctions in ethics, namely, that between conditional and actual oughts, whoever fails here faces an insuperable obstacle to success in developing ethics as a science.

5. Although the following seem hardly worth mentioning, I find that beginning students often fail to differentiate between a value and valuing, between valuing (appreciating) and a value judgment (an assertion about a value), between valuing and evaluating (or valuation and evaluation), between a particular value judgment and a standard for judging, and between values as ends-in-themselves enjoyments and values as approval of conformity with social fads.

Turning now from confusions existing in value theory, discussed above, to additional confusions existing in ethical theory, we select eleven typical problems.

1. Ethics means "Don't." A child's first encounters with "ethics," which may come even in infancy, consist in "Don't do this" and "Don't do that." "Stop it!" "That is something you should *not* do, should *never* do!" Ethical codes, whether familial, play group, educational or religious ("Thou shalt not . . ."), tend to be stated negatively. Thus early and continuingly a child learns that ethics is negative, that its commands are frustrating. Hence, except as he learns to profit by playing the game by prohibiting others, he regards ethics as an evil, something to avoid or escape from if he can.

The falsity of this half-true view of ethics is easy to demonstrate only if one can think through life situations and recondition his firmly established negative conditionings. Ethics is concerned with values, both good and bad, and with maximizing the good and minimizing the bad. It is because there are goods to be achieved or maintained that acts which prevent such achievement or maintenance are right and ought to be performed. When one knows what is best for himself, he naturally seeks it. He does not need to be told. So positive commands are less needed. In fact, they occur usually only after negative encounters, or awareness of danger, appear as "Dont's" that one conceptually and linguistically formulates his "Dos." Surely a science of ethics will seek first the basic goods, and then, or at the same time, the basic evils which endanger the goods. Ethics is concerned with both good and evil, both right and wrong, not with evils and wrongs only, not with goods and rights only. But persistence of the naturally acquired view that ethics is entirely or primarily negative serves as an obstacle to arousing popular interest in developing ethics as a science.

2. "Ethics is what others want me to do, not what I want to do." The "Don't" command of the child's mother comes from outside himself, and frustratingly prevents him from doing what he wants to do. When father, older brother, playmate, teachers, policemen, etc., add to his experience with ethics, what they add always comes from the outside. Western religious instruction reinforces this view by depicting God as outside of man, and even outside of the world: "Ethics is what God wants, not what I want. When what I want is not what God wants, then what I want is sinful and wrong."

The falsity of this less-than-half-true view may be even more difficult to expose. For, as a child grows older, accepts responsibility for himself, for others, for an occupation, wife, children, citizenship, then he hears from others more about what he "ought to" do. Both those interested in his welfare, in his growth and development, and those interested in maintaining or improving his services to them readily tell him what they believe that he "should" do. But all such appeals or commands by others, except those accompanied by force or fear of force, will be effective only if they convince him that his own values are at stake. The ultimate reason why anyone would do anything is that doing will be good or better for him, or, if the options are all bad, then the less or least bad for him. Advice by others who help him to understand what is good, better or best for him is the advice he is most likely to take. Why? Not because they gave it, but because he believes that their advice is correct. If he doubts the views of others, then he tries to think through for himself what is best. When he does, then *he* concludes that he *ought* to do what is best. His oughts are his own. Ultimately, all his oughts are his own; for his obligations to others grow out of his awareness of his need for others and for their help and for doing what is needed in order to promote or continue their help to him. Once awareness of mutuality arises, then one even seeks to do what is good for others also; and then he tends also to seek their advice about what they believe he ought to do. At this point, the advice from others is no longer completely external or outside himself, for after he has drawn others into the circle of his inner friendships, one experiences such advice more as inner than as outer. Although we must delay until later chapters demonstrations of these assertions, the truth is that all oughts have an inner basis and are inner primarily, that some are also outer, and some, for those who have become alienated from their own groups, almost (but not entirely) wholly outer. This view that ethics is what others want, not what I want, establishes an antagonism to ethics which is indeed an obstacle to interest in ethics as a science.

Having mentioned Western religions depicting God as external to men and as condemning men as sinful wrongdoers, I should counter this remark by observing that many Asian religions more wisely locate the ultimate source of value, and thus of rightness, duty and obligation, as inside each person. Such religions are "self-help," not "other-help," religions. Each man's own deficiency hinders him from realizing his own value to its fullest. So it becomes obvious that his basic oughts are all his own. Having spent much time learning about and learning from, and teaching about and advocating learning from Asian philosophies, I must agree with their criticism that Western religion and religious ethics are upsidedown. Of course, to a Westerner, Asians see things upsidedown. No ethical scientist should rest until he has studied all of the world's philosophical resources, and, rejecting also Asian obsolescence and error, until he has tested his conclusions elsewhere. This upsidedown-ness of Western religious ideology is also one of the obstacles to developing interest in ethics as a science.

3. Is ethics individual or social? Here is an issue which should be relatively easy to resolve. Yet deepseated prejudices persist. Let both side be heard.

"Ethics is social, not individual." Although supported by the

view, stated above, that the source of ethics is external to the person, this view claims that the goods, ends or goals sought are also social. More obvious, perhaps, in tribal times when existence seemed more precarious was the almost total dependence of the individual upon his group. When the tribe prospered, the individual prospered by sharing in the goods; when the tribe suffered, whether from famine or war, the individual suffered. Hence group welfare was paramount. Mores were those common behavior patterns which the group believed necessary to its welfare. The etymological relation of the words "ethics" and "morals" to "ethnic" and "mores" testifies to their social origin. Conscience, according to this view, is fear of harming the group, fear that one's disloyalty will be found out, or fear of penalty which the group may impose for violation of its mores.

Recently this view was expressed by students: "By duties I always mean duties to others, not duties to myself. Duty, as what is owed, is always owed to others. It is nonsense to say I owe myself something." "Duties are tasks assigned by groups, and have to do with what a person owes to his group, such as tax assessments, or to other members of his group, such as justice and the civil rights." "Duties are what I owe others; rights are what others owe me. But my rights are social, not private, affairs. Even my right to privacy is a social proclaimed right." Rights, whether provided by constitution or by subsequent legislation, are social in origin. What a person does that is not illegal and does not interfere with the rights of others is his own business and has nothing to do with ethics.

"Ethics is individual, not social." One's choice is always his own. One's intentions are always his own. One's conscience is always his own. One's acts, whether right or wrong, are always his own. One's goods, especially one's intrinsic value or values, are his own. So, all of one's obligations are his own. Ethics is concerned with self-realization, and it is only because a person wants to realize his potentialities as a socialized human being that he, for his own reasons, participates in groups. The problem of how many groups to join, which groups and how much of himself he shall devote to each are more basic, ethically, than group regulations because the latter are completely dependent upon the former. Whether or not

to withdraw from a group or to revolt against a group are also ethical questions. The world's greatest ethical and religious teachers were all rebels who protested against the group-imposed mores of their time. Today, "down with the establishment" anarchists protest that they are the only truly moral, the only genuinely honest people. Their critics inquire, "If you destroy all mores, what will you put in their place? Must you be always destructive, never constructive?" Then anarchists reply, "To construct another organization would merely establish different rules to restrict our moral freedom. All group regulations are wrong. It would be immoral to turn around and organize other groups." Genuine ethics is individual and consists in maintaining freedom of choice. Hence, genuine ethics is individual, not social.

A third view, that individual ethics and social ethics interdepend and supplement each other, will be explored later. Here we merely observe that, so long as this issue remains unsolved, the ardor with which each side is supported inhibits efforts to study ethics scientifically. Some "ethics is social" advocates may fear that snooping researchers will unsettle their mores and create havoc. Some "ethics is individual" advocates may claim that science, with its "repeatable experiment" doctrine, is essentially a social enterprise; if a scientist aims to discover universal principles holding for all ethical situations, this is precisely the kind of thing which moral anarchists are trying to prevent, and, in fact, regard as a moral duty to prevent.

4. "Ethics consists in codes." This view is countered by another: "Ethics consists in principles." A code is made up of commandments, whether revealed, legislated or just now agreed upon. A code is a statement of what one ought to do, at least under certain circumstances. It does not, or it certainly need not, explain why. Principles, on the other hand, are explanatory statements. They serve as reasons why one should or should not act in a certain way. Principles, some say, are much more important than codes because they constitute the bases upon which codes are formulated. If one understands the principles then he does not need the code; codes, no matter how long they become, can never cover all of the cases which come up, so one who knows the principles will know how to act even in the absence of a code and also be able to decide whether

or not the code item applies. But, others retort, codes are more practical. When a person assembles a new machine, what he needs is a set of directions, not a physics textbook. When it comes time to act, one needs a code which can be consulted quickly, or better, one simple enough to keep in mind.

The intricacies of this issue must not detain us here. It is hardly a serious issue, except that so long as people confuse the two, as is so often done, they may remain unclear as to just what a scientific study of ethics can do to help the situation.

5. Some oughts, obligations or duties are actual, others are merely conditional. For example, "If I damage your property, then I ought to pay for the damage," asserts a conditional ought. "I damaged your property; therefore I ought to pay for the damage," asserts an actual ought. On the one hand, this distinction between conditional and actual oughts is simple, clear and obvious. On the other hand, it is usually forgotten; its neglect causes confusion; and this confusion both complicates and blurs ethical situations often in ways which are demoralizing. For example, when property is discovered to be damaged and circumstantial evidence points to me, the owner claims, "You damaged my property. So you ought to pay," stating an ought unconditionally, i.e. asserting that the ought is actual. But, since I am not aware that I caused the damage, I reply, trying to deny that I assent that the ought is actual, even though I admit the ought is conditional. If cool headed, I would reply, "I'm not sure." But when surprised and embarrassed by an accusation of guilt, I reject the accusation, saying, "No. That's not so." Or, if even less critical, I may say, "I ought not!" The owner then interprets my refusal to assent to an actual ought as a denial or even a conditional ought. This makes me appear unreasonable, further antagonizes the owner, and causes him to be more convinced than ever that I am responsible. The damage resulting from the clash of tempers may be worse than the original property damage, not merely by creating distrust between persons but by adding to the annoyance and frustration accompanying dealing with ethical situations.

Furthemore, keeping the distinction clearly in mind is essential to understanding the nature of rules, regulations, laws, standards, advice and commands. Usually rules are intended as statements of conditional oughts. "Drive on the right" ordinarily is intended to connote "if the way is clear." But, when an obstacle appears on the right, then one is expected to pass on the left. The rule as stated remains universal or, at best, indefinite. If one interprets the rule as not merely a universal conditional ought but as a universal actual (called "categorical") ought, then he will stop or slow down when he meets the obstacle, and probably either curse rulemakers or feel that he has acted wrongly in driving on the left. Drivers familiar with such rules are acquainted with their conditional intent. But persons facing rules for the first time, especially in highly technical situations, must tend to regard rules as unconditional until they learn what the conditions are. Much acrimonious disputation has occurred over interpretations of "The Ten Commandments." Is "Thou shalt not kill . . ." a categorical (universal and unconditional actual) or a conditional ought? Or, in more popular language, is it an absolute or merely a relative ought?

Until issues of this sort becomes clear, i.e. that the distinctions between conditional and actual oughts, between universal and merely particular oughts, or between absolute and relative oughts, should be kept in mind at all times, people are likely to believe that it is impossible to develop ethics as a science. Lack of clarity here is, I believe, one of the most serious obstacles to be overcome.

6. What are "ideals"? Are all ideals ethical? Are all ideals oughts? Ought one have "high ideals"? Are ideals conditional or unconditional oughts? Ought one have unrealizable ideals or only realizable ideals? Does having high ideals make one unrealistic or impractical? Is it unrealistic not to have ideals? When ideals conflict, do oughts conflict? Is there some ideal or ought for resolving conflicts between ideals? Can ideals be shared? Are ideals necessarily unchanging or are they changeable? Are ideals standards existing as external compulsions, or do they arise out of the individual as aims depicting unrealized desires?

So long as people are confused about the nature of ideals, they will have doubts as to whether ideals can be dealt with scientifically.

7. What is "conscience"? Is it "the voice of God implanted in each soul," "the voice of the herd, evolved through centuries of biological conditioning," "the voice of a profounder wish-level," a

fear resulting from stimulus-response conditioning, a fear of the invisible power of the group to compel conformity, a fear that one will fail to realize his ideals, or some other, perhaps more complicated, kind of thing?*

Doubts about the nature of conscience serve also as doubts as to whether conscience can be understood scientifically.

8. The word "right" has two commonly used but diametrically opposed meanings. On the one hand, "right" is opposed to "wrong," and "rights" to "wrongs." On the other hand, "a right" is opposed to "a duty," and "rights" to "duties." My action is right when I am doing my duty. When I assert my rights, I am asking others to do their duties to me. No trouble arises when these words are used in different contexts where their respective meanings are clear. But why there should be two such widely differing meanings attached to the same word, and why, further, elementary textbooks usually totally ignore the subject, is another puzzle confronting whoever suggests considering ethics scientifically. It may be trivial to note that "right" is also opposed to "left," except that, when driving in some countries, it is right to drive on the right side of the road while in other countries it is wrong to drive on the right side. "Right" also appears in "right-angled" and in "upright," the latter applying equally well to a verticle post and an "upright citizen." The Spanish word, "derecho," meaning "right" or law," never connotes "rightness" as opposed to "wrongness" so far as I have been able to discover—which points up both additional obstacles where translation between different languages is concerned and the fact that each language and each cultural tradition has its own peculiar kinds of confusions regarding axiology and ethics, all of which an international or universal science of ethics must overcome.

9. "Justice" and "injustice," two of the most widely used terms especially in political and legal ethics, at first seem to have clear and simple meanings. Justice requires equality. But difficulties arise when we discover that people are both alike and unlike in various ways, and that unlikenesses have a way of intruding in social situations. If two persons are unequal, how can you treat them equally

---

*See Theories of conscience. *Ethics,* 75(2):128-131, Jan. 1965.

unless you treat each in a way appropriate to the way he is, i.e. as unequal. A mother and her child are equal in the sense of both being persons; but the mother gave birth to the child and the child cannot reciprocate by giving birth to its mother. The early "eye for an eye, and a son for a son" law of strict justice had to give way to "three cows for a son" because the strict justice principle was clearly unjust to the son. The easily forgotten distinction between distributive and retributive justice, and complications relating them to the disappearance of rights (as when bankruptcy eliminates debts), lead some to believe that the difficulties inherent in understanding justice alone are sufficient to defy success in treating ethics as a science.

10. "Fredom," although not strictly an ethical term, is so closely related to "intention," "volition" and "choice" on the one hand, and to "political liberties" on the other, that few discussions of ethical problems escape using it. Those who believe that acts are right only if voluntary, and that acts are voluntary only if will is free, insist that no science of ethics is possible which fails to understand the nature of freedom. But, since controversies continue to rage over whether freedom means merely absence of restraint, self-determinism, indeterminism, submission of lower to higher interests, accepting oneself as an agent, etc., many dispair that the question will ever be settled. Particularly vicious is the most common view that freedom and determinism are incompatible, implying that in a completely determined world there can be no freedom and therefore no ethics, and that in a world where there is freedom and indeterminism science will be unable to make reliable predictions, and therefore that assertion of freedom implies any attempt to treat ethics as a science must end in futility. Recently in America youthful advocates of freedom from responsibility, or rights without duties and of liberty as license, have gained a hearing, have inspired other youthful converts and have thus produced another obstacle to the kind of open-minded inquiry needed by ethics as a science.

11. Finally, let us recall that each of the several sciences has tended to develop its own views about the nature of ethics, and that each has acquired a vested interest in maintaining its own view. They are, naturally, slanted by the need in each for clarifying for

itself the centrality of its own problems and efforts. Anthropology, sociology, economics, political science, jurisprudence, history, philosophy of religion, philosophy of art, psychology, biology, etc., all deal with ethics. Although most are likely to recognize that in some way or other, ethics is or ought to be foundational to their own subjects, they tend to be much more concerned about their own subjects as contributing to, and thus foundational to, ethics. It is true that each does have a contribution to make. And any adequate science of ethics will recognize and appreciate such contributions. But the emphasis normally given to interpreting ethics from the viewpoint of the specialty, especially if and when expressed dogmatically and as if exclusively the correct view, also adds to the complexities confronting students. A study of such different viewpoints tends to leave the inquirer with a sense of hopelessness that the diversity can ever be overcome, especially if he regards these sciences as already established while ethics is not. Hence, the increase in specialization within each of several other sciences, in ways which depend upon and strengthen or stiffen their biased conception of what constitutes ethics, is itself one major obstacle to be overcome in establishing ethics as a science. Once established with its own primary data and methodology and conclusions, ethics as a science will have a long-enduring task of helping to rectify mistaken elements in the bases of such other sciences.

FAILURES BY PHILOSOPHERS

My harshest criticisms are reserved for philosophers because they, more than any other group, are the responsible custodians of mankind's concern for thinking things through in the realm of values as well as of reality and knowledge. About eight thousand persons now teach philosophy in American colleges. Although some are specialized in other areas, a majority of them have had some training in ethical theory, in the history of ethical theories and in the issues at stake.

Many, of course, have accepted their responsibility and have tried to fulfill their obligations both as students and as teachers. Some of these have begun with sectarian biases which could not be overcome. Some believe that objectivity requires an attitude of neutrality which helps their students to make up their own minds without biasing influences. Some have found that ethical problems cannot be solved apart from epistemological and metaphysical problems and so have become preoccupied with them. Some have achieved synthetic perspective, but seem to be given to defending the peculiarities of their system and of the language in which it is stated so much so that they cannot communicate effectively.

Many others, doubtless a growing quantity, have succumbed to the forces of popular demoralization and have abandoned serious efforts. Some of these have become attracted to particular philosophies condemning the whole philosophical, as well as scientific, enterprise as futile. And some are sophists, never intending to take philosophy seriously, who entered the field for an easy living when vacancies occurred. Some are simply incompetent. Some have family and other practical preoccupations which prevent attention sustainable long enough to do effective work.

But teachers of philosophy are not solely responsible for their predicament. People, other scientists, even administrators do not normally consult professors of ethics when they have ethical problems to solve. Curiously, most people tend to be either satisfied with their own views (if they were not, they would have already given them up in favor of more satisfactory ones) or too embarrassed to reveal their ignorance or uncertainty about such fundamental matters. When philosophers are not called upon to provide reliable answers, their sense of responsibility diminishes. They can retreat to "the ivory tower" with impunity. There they devote attention to problems of their own choosing, or, if they congregate in groups, can be aroused to dispute over technical issues currently disturbing their peer group. But failure to be called upon by the public does not excuse them from their responsibilities. Especially now, in a time of great moral and philosophical turbulence, there is growing need for new answers which point to a new, more widely based, freshly thought-through *weltanschauung*.

In what follows, I hope to illustrate how the failures of philosophers, aggravated by the failure of people to make demands upon philosophers, serve as obstacles to furthering ethics as a science.

Selected for mention are: (1) difficulties encountered in studying and teaching ethics; (2) tendencies to subordinate issues in ethics to those in other fields such as metaphysics, epistemology, logic; (3) examples of negative influences by notable historical and contemporary philosophies; and (4) the chaotic, ineffective, debilitating status of professional philosophy.

1. Difficulties encountered in studying and teaching ethics. Many of these are common to all fields of philosophy: lack of standardized courses, textbooks, aims, terminology and even agreements about the nature and limits of the subject. Lack of minimum standards is discouraging to beginning students who tend to give up if they do not acquire a somewhat satisfactory grasp of the subject early. Even in absence of disagreement, writers on ethics may confuse students by their choice of words. For example, recently a student cited two authors as saying ethics is the science (1) "of the ideal involved in human life" and (2) "of moral character." He interpreted these as conflicting definitions, complaining that "our first problem arises in a concrete form of seeking a definition of ethics." The subject is so complex that one may choose any of the several key terms, each of which entails all of the others, without contradiction. But this is not evident to beginners. Hence, some attention to the problem of how to teach ethics and of how to teach philosophy is needed. Such attention is almost completely lacking in the training of philosophy teachers in the United States.

One comparative difficulty for college teachers is that neither philosophy nor ethics is taught in most high schools. Neither students nor teachers face the same difficulties when students have been introduced to their subject already in high school. However, since other difficulties are more basic, shifting introductions to ethical theory to lower grades will not solve, but may even aggravate, them. The subject is sufficiently complex and important that each university should have a distinct department of ethics, not just a course or two in a department of philosophy.

Shall a teacher start with practical problems (students tend to focus on details and resist efforts to detect and clarify principles), or with principles (students find these dry, uninteresting), or with history of theories (creates misconception that ethics consists in history of theories), or yield to the temptation to indoctrinate one viewpoint (students feel imposed upon)? Confronted with such difficulties, many teachers and students avoid courses in ethics; and where colleagues distrust each other, each may try to prevent the other from teaching the course. Consequently, also the lack of such courses may itself be a cause of lack of attention to developing ethics as a science.

2. Issues in ethics tend to be subordinated to those in other fields. This problem has three aspects.

a. Some problems in ethics are intimately interrelated with those of metaphysics, epistemology, logic, social philosophy, religion, etc. Since such ethical problems cannot be solved adequately until these other problems are solved, delay in understanding and teaching them must be expected. So ethicists are drawn into work in other fields. Hence the status of ethics is handicapped by lack of development in the field of philosophy as a whole, which in turn is dependent upon lack of development in each of the many fields including ethics.

b. Some problems plaguing students and teachers of ethics are really problems centering in other fields. To mention only one, yielding to the temptation to interpret opposites as contradictories (e.g. rights-duties, is-ought, freedom-determinism) results from inadequate teaching of logic, which may result from failure to develop logic as a science. A student of ethics, seeking to be logical, often assumes that there is only one way to be logical and only one logic. Although, ultimately, this is the case, none of the logics formulated thus far appears to be ultimate in the sense of being completely adequate. The current flare of symbolic logic, despite its use in reshaping mathematics teaching and the elegance of its technical proofs, has had a crippling effect on popular interest in, and competence in, logic. The extreme abstractness and distance from practical experience, the adoption of "material implication" and an extreme doctrine of external relatedness, and the formal intricacy of commonly employed inferences, all cause practical-minded students to lose interest quickly, especially when teachers lack patience to lay the groundwork and to keep its extremely limited utility continually in mind. The temptation to display brilliance in grappling with technical paradoxes seems irresistable. The fact that new devices with new assumptions work with greater elegance has been used mistakenly to downgrade traditional and, popularly, more useful logic. And preoccupation with problems, inherent in symbolic systems has prevented looking at Jain, Buddhist, Hindu and Chinese logics, to say nothing of ignoring dialectical and pragmatic logics. Failure to develop logic as a science and to teach logic effectively is a part of the trouble which needs to be overcome before ethics as a science can flourish. How much of New Left anarchistic "down with everything" (including ethics) motives result from failure in effective teaching of logic, or even merely from failure to teach logic?

c. Not only does ethics depend upon solutions in other fields, not only do ethicists become drawn away from ethical problems to work on problems in other fields, and not only do failures in other fields effect, and mistakenly appear as, failures in ethics, but also each of these tends to have its own biased perspective of ethical problems and solutions. That is, not only do the physical, biological and social sciences each understand ethics in terms of their own problems and perspectives, but also each of the philosophical sciences does the same.

Metaphysics is concerned primarily with the nature of existence, not with values and obligations, except that these too must exist. Excluding those metaphysical schemes which assume purpose or personality as ultimate, the role of value and obligation is often deduced from metaphysical assumptions rather than based on primary data. Epistemology, or theory of knowledge, truth and certainty, has so much trouble with knowledge of physical things, sensations, appearances, memory, the future, self and universals that the seemingly still-more-difficult knowledge of values and obligations tends to be postponed and neglected. Logic, as a science of structure, should be as much concerned with value structures as any others, but has come to be regarded as completely sterilized of values. Philosophy of religion, although intimately interdependent with axiology and ethics, has been saddled with culturally inherited theistic revelations, and consequently has tended to subordinate ethics to theology. Political and social philosophies, which might have been expected to settle value and moral questions first, in fact tend to focus on group welfare, social control, organization of authority and power, and political rights and duties, and to deduce what characters and values persons must have in order to play their social roles. Even aesthetics, preoccupied with multitudes of problems in the philosophy art, and of each of the arts, tends to exclude concerns about ethics, except when forced to recognize ethical assmuptions involved in problems or standards of artistic criticism. Philosophy of language, currently popular, although occasionally helping to clarify some ethical terms, has had the effect of reducing problems in ethics to problems in language; especially notorious are those who adopt criteria of meaning which exclude values and obligations from having meaning, thus declaring all problems in axiology and ethics as meaningless. In sum, every other field of philosophy has its own way of subordinating ethics and thus of presenting a somewhat derogatory and sometimes false view of ethics.

Failure on the part of philosophers, especially of those embodying the specialized perspectives of its particular branches, to recognize the basic nature and importance of ethics is a continuing factor among the difficulties encountered in developing ethics as a science.

3. Examples of negative influences by notable philosophies upon the development of ethics as a science. Space permits neither adequate exposition of the philosophies nor demonstration of our assertions. Doubtless search will reveal some persons who, although starting from the typical viewpoints criticized below, have made efforts in the direction of developing ethics as a science. Selected for mention are Thomism, Materialism, Spiritualism, Positivism, Linquistic Analysis, Existentialism, Phenomenology, Hinduism, Buddhism, Taoism and Confucianism.

Thomism, although advocating ethics as a science, does so in the sense of an organized body of knowledge which it subordinates to theology and revelation. Many Thomistic ethicists have made astute observations about human nature and its moral nature and needs. Yet, in the end, theological and revelational preconceptions have restricted, and in this sense have prevented, searching for the initial foundations of a science of ethics in human behavior. Recent new revolts within the Roman Catholic Church indicate increasing dissatisfaction with authoritarianism; but Thomism itself embodies static preconceptions which, if accepted, discourage investigating and adopting dynamic conceptions.

Mechanistic materialism, interpreting man as a machine in which values appear, accidentally, unnecessarily, gratuitously, as momentary pleasures or, at best, satisfactions of biological instincts, regards physics and physiological psychology as sufficient to account for man's behavior and sees no need for a separate science of ethics with its own basic problems, data and conclusions.

Spiritualism regards the spiritual, and each man as spirit, as unitary and unique, and hence not interpretable by universals or science. One intuits his identity with ultimate reality and value, so science is unnecessary. Some spiritualists interpret spirit as rational, and these tend to develop ethics as a deductive science. But then the ethical becomes subordinated to the rational, and the necessity often claimed for moral commands (e.g. Immanuel Kant's "categorical imperative") is a rational rather than a moral necessity. Thus far, spiritualisms, whether rationalistic or antirationalistic, have contributed little toward ethics as a behavioral science.

Positivism, or rather logical positivism, claims that science is factually descriptive and that all value and ethical statements are emotive. Its criterion of meaning is such that all value statements are meaningless. Hence no science of values or of ethics is possible. Some linguistic analysts claim that the sole purpose of philosophy is to analyze and clarify the meanings of terms. To propose hypotheses about existence, including the existence of values, is not its business. Hence, it provides no basis for an appeal to ethics as a science.

Existentialism, locating ultimate reality and value (*existenz*) in spontaneous will, claims that each person's whatness (essence) is, at least when he is "authentic," solely a product of his own will. When one person permits any act of will to be imposed upon by others (whereby he is "treated as an object"), by machines, by social laws or mores, or by rules of logic, or even by his own previously willed commitments, he becomes "inauthentic." Since "inauthenticity" is the greatest evil, all restrictions by science should be avoided when possible. Hence, Existentialism, so interpreted, is essentially antiscientific, and thus opposed to encouraging ethics as a science.

Phenomenology, although related to Existentialism, opens the door to values as needs of men and seeks to formulate a new phenomenological, i.e. subjective, science of values. But, since it explicitly and systematically postpones (i.e. "brackets") all questions about the real world, in effect, it excludes treating ethics as a realistic science or a science of human behavior in the ordinary sense of this term. The science it seeks must be regarded as a semi-science, or a semi-sufficient science. However, since its doctrine of "bracketing" indicates that it remains open to changing its mind later, its effect is to postpone rather than to repress efforts toward developing ethics as a behavioral science.

Looking to India, where ideas of *karma* and *dharma* prevail, one might expect to find support for ethical generalizations. Yet these tend to be subordinated to ideals of ultimate reality, *nirvana,* as purified of all distinctness, definiteness and uniformity of the sort science seeks. Yogins seek to transcend ethical considerations as quickly as possible through mystical, rather than scientific, means. Buddhism, although originating in a basic moral insight of Gotama, the Buddha, evolved through Theravada ("impermanence"), Sunyavada ("voidness"), Zen ("satori"), and Shin (salvation by grace) doctrines, none of which favors science as a mode of inquiry. The net effect of Buddhism is anti-scientific and, indeed, anti-ethical, since quick transcendence of the ethical is its aim.

Looking to China, Taoism as naturalism at first seems to offer no obstacles until it is recognized that science is regarded as artificial. Nature operates from within; science as conclusions about laws for guidance of conduct operates from without. Confucius, not merely a moralist but, in a sense, the first moral scientist, centered his teachings about man's social nature. His ideas and ideals, summarized by *yi, jen, li* and *chih,** doubtless will be confirmed by any mature science of ethics. But centuries of transmissions have formalized Confucianism, and reverence for the text, uncertain as it is, has tended to make the followers of Confucius

---

*See the following books by this author: *The Heart of Confucius* (New York, Weatherhill, 1969), Introduction; *Tao Teh King by Lao Tzu* (New York, Ungar, 1958), pp. 107-119; and *The World's Living Religions* (Carbondale, Ill., Southern Illinois University Press, 1971), pp. 177-191.

more authoritarian, or merely moralistic, than scientific in their attitudes.

4. The chaotic, ineffective, debilitating status of professional philosophy. Although many earnest, able, sound and effective individual teachers of philosophy enlighten, inform and inspire today, the multiplicity of doctrines, traditional and novel, taught in the name of academic freedom creates an impression that philosophy is an area where anyone has license to say anything he pleases, whether responsibly or not. As philosopher, one should remain open-minded, and as teacher one should arouse curiosity and explore problems by presenting alternative views fairly. Yet, as both philosophies and conflicts between them multiply, too many teachers yield to the temptation to use their freedom as license to preach bias. Except for the tendency of students and teachers to demonstrate acquaintance with those doctrines currently popular in their peer groups, as well as with favored historical views, diversity prevails.

Increasing numbers of teachers appear to be succumbing to currently popular anarchistic tendencies to which both Existentialist and Linguistic Analysis schools contribute in various ways. When writers vie with each other in claiming that some heretofore valued idea "rests on a mistake," student morale withers. When students are urged not to find life meaningful because life itself has no meaning, but to create meaning spontaneously at will, whimsical bias becomes thereby idealized. Withered morale is being revived as personal bias. Former ideals of seeking understanding, of seeking objectivity and fairness, of seeking truth have almost vanished. Now it is easy to find adherents for the views that philosophy itself rests on a mistake and that philosophy is whatever you wish at the moment to make it. For such people, philosophy is no longer a quest for wisdom. In such a melieu, to advocate devotion to developing ethics as a science is to be out of line, except as another variety of willful bias.

Instead of belaboring further deficiencies—such as the failure to establish a society of American ethicists when specialized societies have been organized for all other branches of philosophy; the failure to achieve a Nobel prize award by American philosophers, let alone ethicists; the failure of philosophers to share in lucrative research grants; the failure of philosophers to be hailed as leaders—let me here express my own hope. Progressive erosion of traditional ideals and increasingly violent anarchistic cries push demoralization toward an ultimate limit of meaninglessness from which life will rebel and rebound. Nothing is so powerful as a need whose time for fulfillment has come. Let us hope that it will lead us not on some wild and willful venture, *á la* Nietzsche, Hitler or Sartre, and not into some totalitarian straitjacket, *á la* Mussolini or Marx, but will somehow combine the sanity of a Lao Tzu, the wisdom of a Socrates and a Gotama, the love of a Jesus, the patience of a Gandhi, the opposites-synthesizing ability of a Hegel, the insight into dynamic intricacies of a Whitehead and the practicality of a Dewey.

While philosophers and other humanists are wallowing in debility, philosophy is being taught in other departments. Every working man needs, knows he needs, and presupposes that he has, ethics, and that his own views are justified on some basis even though he has not figured them out in detail. Medicine, architecture, city planning, engineering, atomic science and social welfare specialists tend to accept and operate upon principles which demoralized philosophers now repudiate. Systems engineering, emerging explosively to meet demands for computer programming, has become a new science presupposing wholistic and humanitarian principles; when philosophers refuse to supply their needs, they do not stop operating, but rather develop their own philosophies in ways consistent with their own problems and procedures. Special systems theories have been generalized into "general systems theory" (a new name for philosophy) which is then used both to organize and criticize various "belief systems" (another name for particular philosophies). The needs of systems engineers for workable insights into ethical systems will be serviced, whether ably or poorly, regardless of whether or not philosophers assist. Lack of philosophical training and experience is an obstacle handicapping systems theorists. Lack of willingness on the part of humanists to subordinate themselves to the supposed dehumanizing demands of the "military-industrial-university complex" is a two-sided obstacle, handicapping systems theorists and squandering an opportunity to help guide a new intellectual and moral development and in ways which prevent the establishment of new biases naturally arising out of engineering practices.

CHURCH-CONNECTED HINDRANCES

Orthodox Christianity accepts the existence of God, divinely revealed scriptures expressing the will of God as the Word of God, in ways which are believed to be true and adequate for both religious and moral guidance. Nothing more is needed. The Bible contains not only the well-known Ten Commandments, but also hundreds of rules in the Old Testament, the teachings of the Prophets, the teachings of Jesus summing up all commandments as two, i.e. love God whole-heartedly and love your neighbor as yourself, and the teachings of Paul and the Apostles. Devotion to developing ethics as a science is discouraged, because either its conclusions are exactly the same as those of the Bible, in which case it is superfluous, or its conclusions differ from those of the Bible, in which case they are false.

The Roman Catholic Church, after being influenced by Aristotelian and Thomistic philosophy, accepted as aids the Thomistic conceptions of ethics as a science because there were purportedly demonstrated to be expositions of, deductions from, or at least consistent with, authorized doctrine. After many centuries of development in the astronomical, physical, chemical, biological, physiological and historical sciences, the Hierarchy of Bishops grudgingly conceded that many Biblical statements could not be accepted literally. But, despite developments in psychology, anthropology, sociology, ethics and philosophy of religion, Catholic clergy still maintain that "the infallible teaching authority of the Church extends to all matters appertaining to faith and morals."* Empirical or experimental science, if it "disregards the idea of original sin because it holds man to be naturally good or, at the worst, morally neutral," is rejected. "The absence of absolutes of any kind and the concepts of morals as relative and adaptable to environment repu-

---

*W. Wilmers, *Handbook of the Christian Religion,* 3rd ed. (New York, Benziger Brothers, 1891, 1982), p. 132.

diate a morality based on the divine law."† Hence, the Roman
Catholic Church, with its vast army of priests and teachers, apparently opposes, discourages and, if and when it can, tries to prevent
development of ethics as a behavioral science. Contemporary
rebellious protests by many Catholic priests may lead to changes
in the Church's position, but they have had no serious effect yet.

The Protestant Reformation resulted in many independent church
bodies, rejecting Papal authority but keeping the main doctrines.
John Calvin's *Institutes of the Christian Religion,* 24, states that

> The use of the Moral Law is threefold. The first shows us our
> weakness, unrighteousness, and condemnation; not that we may
> despair, but that we may flee to Christ. The second is, that those
> who are not moved by promises, may be urged by the terror of
> threatenings. The third is that we may know what is the will of
> God; that we may consider it in order to obedience; that our minds
> may be strengthened for that purpose; and that we may be kept
> from falling.

Martin Luther's doctrine of total depravity of man, who can be
saved only by the grace of God in whose mercy we must have
faith, has no place for science either. In later centuries, after scientific discoveries became widely known, many accepted the view
that, since God created the world, whatever truths scientists discover about the world are really truths about God's world and
hence there can be no inconsistency between the two truths. In this
way, some orthodox interpreters approved scientific investigations;
but when the truths discovered by scientists conflicted with those
in the Bible, some rejected the Bible and some rejected science.
Members of some churches, Methodists for example, differ peace-
fully on whether or not to promote science. Yet, as long as ministers
use the orthodox scriptures as primary bases for their teachings, the
main effect of their efforts is to direct attention away from, rather
than toward, ethics as a science.

Current stirrings of the "God is dead" movement, Christian Existentialism, "Situation Ethics" and radical reformers in the Catholic
Church, all appear to be revolts against tradition in the direction
of personal freedom and social welfare. They are not science-ward,

---

†*New Catholic Encyclopedia* (New York, McGraw-Hill, 1967), vol. V, p. 756.

generally speaking. Although many eulogize the values of science in increasing our standards of living, longevity, health and education, I have heard no cries from any of these sources that we should seek to develop a science of religion and a science of ethics first and then base our religious and ethical beleifs and practices upon them. Thus, while decline in the rigidity of orthodoxy might be expected to reduce church opposition to pursuing ethics as a science, the consequent arousing and focusing of attention on other issues has thus far provided little benefit.

CONCLUSION

The foregoing survey of obstacles is far from complete. Even if all of the aforementioned obstacles were removed and even if ethical scientists had already reached desired conclusions, would men automatically accept them? Some say that the power of personal habits and the power of social mores are so strong that few could break their habits and adopt new ones. Each person and each group has vested interests in its established working structures. Ethical scientists could expect improvement only by beginning with children. If the rest of us are unlikely to benefit, why should we bother ourselves about promoting ethics as a science? Thus recognizing that a science of ethics, even if successful in achieving the desired understanding, would have little immediate practical value is itself a significant kind of obstacle.

CHAPTER 2

WAYS IN WHICH ALL ETHICAL SITUATIONS ARE ALIKE

PROBABLY the most common objection to ethics as a science is that each ethical situation is particular, unique and different from all others, whereas science deals only with universals, uniformities or likenesses. The most effective way to refute this objection is to point out ways in which all ethical situations are alike. The purpose of the present chapter is to call attention to some of these ways in a systematic manner.

Before beginning, two previously mentioned confused distinctions need to be recalled:

1. The objection is based on a confusion which may be described in various ways: confusion of theory with practice, of science with engineering, or of pure science with applied science. The scientist (or "pure scientist"), seeking to understand, studies his subject matter for the purpose of formulating a theory about uniformities. The engineer (or "applied scientist"), seeking to solve a particular practical problem, uses theories supplied by the scientist as aids. Ethics, as a science (i.e. as a pure science), has as its task the understanding of uniformities or likenesses involved in ethical situations and to formulate theories about them. As a pure science, ethics finishes its task when it understands all such uniformities and when it formulates and finishes testing theories about them.

2. A second distinction, this one between actual and conditional oughts, is based on the first one. By "conditional ought" is meant something which one ought to do *if* all of certain specified conditions occur.

Recalling our previous example, we remember that water has a certain boiling point, and that if we desire to boil water, we must heat it to that point. Apparently, physical scientists have established as a principle or law (i.e. a theory considered proved) that water boils at 212° F under certain conditions, such as at sea level under normal atmospheric pressure. Notice that such a principle serves as a basis for a conditional ought. That is, "If I wish to boil water at sea level under normal atmospheric pressure, then I ought to heat it to 212° F." Such conditional ought is stated as a universal. That is, "I always ought to heat water to 212° F, if I wish to boil it at sea level under normal atmospheric pressure." Whenever one stops to think about it, he realizes that the permanent universality of the physicist's principle serves permanently as a basis for a permanent universal conditional ought. But such a conditional ought is not an actual ought. Merely as conditional, it does not assert that I do, I want to or that I ought to want to boil water, either now or at any time.

On the other hand, if it is true that I am at sea level under normal atmospheric pressure and have some water and the means of heating it and that I do want to boil it now, then it is true that I do have an actual ought, namely, "I ought to heat this water to 212° F now." This actual ought is a particular, unique ought. It is occurring here and now under present conditions, including my present desire and the presumed universal truth of the physicist's principle. The conditional ought participates in the becoming of an actual ought if and when all of the necessary conditions are fulfilled.

Ethical practice (ethics as an applied science, or ethical engineering) consists in confronting actual oughts, with or without awareness of conditional oughts. Some actual oughts arise so suddenly and compellingly that reflection is impossible. If one has acquired habits of thought or action which suggest to him a best course of action automatically, he may observe his actual ought and act as he ought quickly and without reflection (as one commonly does in riding a bicycle or driving a car). When one is aware that he will be facing certain typical obligations, then ought he not prepare in advance to become acquainted with the relevant principles and their consequent conditional oughts and acquire habits of being alert to discovering his actual oughts and of quickly doing as he actually ought? Driver training programs, for example, are designed to aid persons to discover principles, laws, conditional oughts and habits of thought and action relative to them.

Ethics as a pure science is concerned only with universal principles, and most, if not all, of these will be found to be conditional oughts.

The purpose of the present chapter, more fully stated, is (1) to survey some of the many ways in which all ethical situations are alike, and to do so sufficiently to convince some skeptics that there are, if not more likenesses than differences, then at least enough likenesses to remove doubts about being able to generalize about them scientifically; and (2) to call attention to the fact that all such likenesses may serve as bases for conditional oughts and that, therefore, all of the developments in all of the sciences are, in this sense, already developments in ethics as a science. From this viewpoint, ethics is an already well-established science, and the ethicist should seek to encourage developments in all other sciences because they also serve as developments in ethics as a science.

In attempting to organize the vast multitude of scientific laws in some managable way so as to illustrate the many different types relevant to ethical situations, I have adopted the following outline:

1. Those universals or likenesses common to all existing situations (and therefore common also to all ethical situations); e.g. those dealt with in metaphysics and the physical sciences.

2. Those universals common to all living situations (and therefore common to all ethical situations); e.g. those dealt with in the biological sciences.

3. Those universals common to all mental situations (and therefore common to all ethical situations). Omitted here are universals common to all value situations because these are reserved for the next section; e.g. the various psychological and epistemological sciences.

4. Those universals common to all social situations (and therefore common to all ethical, or at least all social, ethical situations); e.g. those dealt with in the social sciences.

5. Those universals common to all value situations (and therefore common to all ethical situations); e.g. axiology, aesthetics and philosophy of religion. Fuller treatment is reserved for the following chapter on axiology or theory of values.

6. Those universals common to all ethical situations. Fuller treatment is reserved for later chapters on individual ethics and social ethics.

It should be noted that, in all of the above types, the question of whether what one scientist proposes or claims to be a universal is one actually, remains open (as part of the scientific attitude, in any case). The examples cited below have been selected somewhat arbitrarily, perhaps somewhat accidentally, and with the intention of serving as illustrative of hypotheses rather than as final dogmas. Furthermore, the issue of whether the universal or law mentioned is actually something common to all situations of the type under consideration or only common to all of some major part or kind of the situations is something which we may not always be clear about. We intend to defer to the specialists in each field concerning such matters. We should be warned also that, since the subject matters of the various sciences overlap, interpenetrate and may be multileveled, our organizational outline, insofar as it suggests certain sciences as primary representatives of one type, may only roughly approximate the actual situation. Likewise, we here give little attention to the fact that each general science has many subsciences, some of which may deal with relatively universal aspects of the type while others may deal with parts of subparts of the area.

METAPHYSICAL AND PHYSICAL SCIENCES

Metaphysics is that science which has as its task the attempt to understand the nature of existence. Using the term "category" to mean characteristics which are universal in all existing things or situations, metaphysics is a study of existence and its categories. If the metaphysician has done his work well (with the help of specialists in all other sciences), his conclusions will be accepted by all others, for each characteristic which is present in all things or situations is present in every physical, chemical, biological, social, economic, epistemological, aesthetic and ethical thing or situation.

To test conclusions about characteristics as metaphysical is, in principle, more difficult than testing characteristics as universal within any less extensive science, since such a test must include tests within all such other sciences also. Hence, in general, a metaphysician needs to keep an open mind about his hypotheses or conclusions longer, perhaps, than does a scientist in the less extensive sciences. Thus, any list of characteristics proposed as metaphysical should be understood as hypothetical and as subject to much more testing. Neither exposition nor testing of proposals about universal characteristics, in any of the sciences, is possible here.

The following list is my own, and has the peculiarity that most, if not all, metaphysical characteristics occur in pairs of opposites. (1) Sameness-difference: All existences are alike in some sense, e.g. alike in being existences and in embodying all of the categories of existence. All existences are different in some sense, e.g. at least each existent is different from every other existent in whatever sense it is not the other. (2) Whole-parts: Each existent or existing situation is in some sense a whole and has parts of some sort or other. No matter how short the event or how long the duration, surely there must be some whole of it and some parts of it. (3) Unity-plurality: No wholeness without unity; no parts without plurality. (4) Relations; internal-external: Each existent is re-lated to some or all other existents at least externally, i.e. in whatever sense each is not the others. Each involves internal re-latedness, both in whatever sense all of its own parts are internal to it and in whatever sense it is the same as, or participates in some larger whole of, any or all other existents. (5) Universal-particular: Each existent is like all others, at least in existing and in embodying all of the categories of existence. Each existent is particular and unique in whatever sense it is different from all others. (6) Changing-permanent: To change is to become different. Each becoming different in any sense in a change. Each existent or existing situation (event) changes, either in the sense of coming into being or going out of being or becoming different, at least by being in or at a different time. To remain the same is to be permanent. Each thing or event is permanent in the sense that it remains through change, or at least as long as it takes for it to occur. Some events remain, endure or are permanent for only very short periods. (7) Old-new. (8) Effect-cause. (9) Substance-function. (10) Actual-potential. (11) Finished-unfinished. (12) End-means. (13) Immanent-transcendent. (14) Thing-space. (15) Kind-degree. (16) Definite-indefinite. (17) Equal-unequal. (18) Dependent-independent. (19) Polar-absolute. (20) Being-dialectical.*

If the above-proposed categories of existence are in fact characteristics common to all existing situations, then they are common to all ethical situations. That is, every ethical situation is in some sense like and in some sense different from all other ethical situations as well as from all other existing situations. Every ethical situation is in some sense a whole and has parts of some sort or other. Each is in some sense a unit and is in some sense plural. Each is in some sense externally related to all other ethical situations and all other situations and has internal relatedness both in the sense that its parts are its own and in whatever sense it is the same as or participates in some larger whole. Each is universal in whatever sense it is like all others and particular and unique in whatever sense it is different from all others. It changes in the sense that it comes into being and goes out of being and is permanent in the sense that it endures or remains through change at least long enough for it to happen. Each is in some sense old and in some sense new; in some sense an effect and in some sense a cause; in some sense substantial and in some sense functional, etc.

If each of the foregoing proposed characteristics is common to every ethical situation, then each may serve as a basis for one or more conditional oughts. That is, if every ethical situation is both

---

Philosophy, An Introduction (Bombay, Asia, 1964), Ch. 20.

Existence and its polarities. *The Journal of Philosophy, 46*(20):629-637, Sept. 29, 1949.

Matter and spirit: Implications of the organicist view. *Philosophy and Phenomenological Research, 18*(4):451-543, June 1958.

Organicism: The philosophy of interdependence. *International Philosophical Quarterly, 7*(2):251-253; 256-262, June 1967.

Polarity, Dialectic, and Organicity (Springfield, Ill., Thomas, 1970).

in some sense a whole and in some sense a thing with parts, then other things being equal, one ought always to regard each ethical situation as in some sense a whole and in some sense as having parts. And, if every ethical situation is in some sense caused and is in some sense a cause, then, other things being equal, one ought always to regard each ethical situation as in some sense caused and in some sense a cause, etc. That is, in whatever ways any ethical situation is or has characteristics which are common to all ethical situations, because common to all existing situations, then those ways serve as a basis for conditional universal oughts. To whatever extent the above categories of existence and conditional oughts have been established, is not ethics as a science already established? And to whatever extent they, and other proposed categories of existence, have not been established, does not an ethicist have a stake in the promotion of metaphysical research and in its pursuit to any possible final conclusions?

Physics is the science which investigates the nature of matter and energy (or "mattergy") and their properties and actions, including such things as motion, light, heat, sound, electricity, magnetism, and now subatomic particles, radioactivity, relativity, etc. Matter has three states (solids, having volume and shape with molecules in fixed positions; liquids, having volume but not shape and with molecules in contact but able to slide around each other; and gases, having neither volume nor shape with molecules free to move in all directions), occupies space, has inertia (resisting starting when at rest and stopping when in motion), has mass (unchanging except by conversion into energy), has weight (depending on gravitational attraction) and has density (or ratio between mass and volume).

Mechanics is that branch of physics concerned with motions of matter and with equilibrium. Force, defined in terms of acceleration, causing a body to move and how much it accelerates the body's motion are always proportional to each other, according to one of Newton's Laws of Motion. Momentum, or the quantity of motion measured by the product of mass and velocity, involves the idea of energy. Energy, whether the kinetic of moving bodies or the potential of stationary bodies, can be neither created nor destroyed, according to the principle of the conservation of energy. Force is of two sorts: weight which is the force of gravity and does not require contact, and friction resulting from contact of two bodies offering resistance to each other. Lubricants reduce friction.

Hydraulics accepts Archimedes' principle that buoyant forces of a liquid are equal to the weight of the liquid displaced. Electromagnetics is concerned with radiant waves, whether of heat, light, radio, ultraviolet, x-rays, gamma rays or cosmic rays. According to nuclear physics, matter in motion is transformed into energy in accordance with the formula $E = mc^2$ (energy = mass times velocity squared), and when the motion attains the speed of light all of it will be transformed.

If the above-listed statements refer to the actual world, as physicists say they do, and if there are no existing situations without matter, energy or gravitation, solids, liquids or gases, and radiation of waves or rays, then these are all present in every ethical situation, and all of the laws pertaining to them hold in such situations. That is, there are no ethical situations without matter and energy, either that within persons or that outside persons. There are no ethical situations where one can violate the principle that two pieces of matter cannot occupy the same space at the same time, or that for each action there is an equal and oposite reaction, or where the law of gravitation does not operate. There are no ethical situations from which are absent space, time and change. That is, all ethical situations are alike in having all of the universal laws of physics operating in them. Those who say that ethical situations are completely unlike each other ignore all of these likenesses.

If every universal law of physics operates in every ethical situation, then each such law serves as a basis for one or more conditional oughts. If the buoyant force of a liquid is equal to the weight of the liquid which is displaced, then when deciding how many can safely ride in a boat, one ought not load it with more weight than the weight of the water displaced. If one wishes to reduce the friction between two bodies, then he ought to apply an appropriate lubricant. If one's body stays in the rays of sunlight or of x-rays too long it will be burned; therefore, if one seeks not to be burned, then he ought not to stay in sunlight or x-rays too long. If mass is transformed into energy completely at the speed of light, then one seeking to survive when traveling in a spaceship ought not to try to travel at the speed of light.

Chemistry, a science concerned especially with the composition of matter and the kinds of energy, is best known for its table of elements arranging more than one hundred different kinds of atoms according to atomic weights and valences relative to oxygen and hydrogen. Atoms combine to form molecules and molecules combine to form mixtures or compounds. Atoms are composed of as many as thirty-five different kinds of subatomic particles, such as electrons, protons, neutrons and positrons. Even without considering new discoveries occurring at explosive rates, the number of different kinds of chemicals is an astounding quantity. Several million organic compounds are known already. Regarding the transformations which occur, multitudes of laws have already been discovered. To cite a single illustration, Charles' Law states that at constant pressure, the volume of a definite weight of gas is directly proportional to its absolute temperature. This law serves as a basis for several conditional oughts; for example, if you heat gas in a closed container too much it will explode; hence, to avoid danger of flying glass, one ought not throw capped bottles into a hot fire.

Two observations are worth noting. First, each of these multitudes of kinds of chemicals has its own nature and laws and thus serves as a basis for conditional oughts. So we should observe how far ethics as a science already has bases for such oughts already established. Secondly, observe both the complexity of the field and of some chemical situations and the diversity of the kinds of chemical situations. The amazing complexity, of the field and of particular compounds, has not stopped scientists from trying to, and succeeding very well, in understanding them. So the argument of those who assert that ethical situations cannot be dealt with because they are too complex seems refuted thereby. The amazingly diversity of things so different as solids, liquids and gases, as acids and alkalies, as a drop of water and a mountain, has not prevented chemists from discovering that they are, nevertheless, all alike in certain respects, such as being composed of atoms, subatomic particles and quanta of energy, with some laws common to all chemical situations. So the argument that vastness of kinds of differences apparent in different ethical situations need not, merely by themselves, preclude successful treatment by scientific methods.

Not all chemicals exist in every ethical situation, but some do. Oxygen, hydrogen, carbon atoms, molecules of water and all chemical essentials to life are present in every living situation, including those needed in the environment, such as the atmosphere, of living beings. Thus, at least the chemical laws involved in the nature of such necessary chemicals are present in every ethical situation. Hence the conditional oughts based on them are relevant to every ethical situation.

Astronomy, geology and *physical geography* also study ever-present conditions of life. Astronomy, in studying the stars, planets, Milky Way, galaxies and their movements and patterns, reveals not only the vastness and complexity of the universe but also both the relative permanence and also the precariousness of human existence on earth. Except for astronautical adventures, men are earthbound and so are all ethical situations. Studies of the solar system show us why we have warm days and cool nights, and have them constantly. Geology, in studying the structure of the earth, has revealed the origin and nature of oceans and continents, of mountains, rivers, valleys, lakes, plains, deserts, caves, the upheavals and erosions, and the distribution of igneous and sedimentary layers of rock with minerals, coal, oil, gas, water, etc., which serve as resources for human life. Although these differ in detail around the globe, each kind of condition has its own nature and laws to which men must adjust if they are to survive. Among the more obvious conditions are the atmospheric and climatic variations in temperature, humidity, atmospheric pressure, wind and rain. Except where men, responding to needs, have succeeded in building shelters, few ethical situations are freed from climatic conditions and their variations. Physical geography, further pursuing geological studies, maps the earth's surface in detail, reveals areas of danger and of fertility, and increasingly shows how men can adjust to and exploit earth's resources and how earth conditions were favorable to the origin and evolution of life and of man. This story is continued by human geographers as well as biologists and anthropologists.

Again, each variation—astronomical, geological or geographical —presents an adjustment challenge to men, though discovery of each variety of condition and of the laws peculiar to it again serve as bases for conditional oughts. There are also some invariant kinds of conditions, such that no person is ever free from being in the Milky Way; in our solar system; on our earth (astronauts excepted); at some place, under gravitational, atmospheric, climatic conditions; and at some time (in the year-month-day cycles). Each of these invariant conditions is subject to invariant laws, and all of these laws serve as ever-present bases for conditional oughts, because they are conditions present in every ethical situation.

For example, if one is planning a trip, then if such astronomical factors as time of sundown on March 1 at 20 degrees latitude, and the day of the month, have a bearing on travel conditions, then one interested in travel safety and efficiency ought to take them into consideration in making his decisions. If the trip is through territory subject to rapid erosion by rain, rivers and underground seepage, then one ought to consult geologists familiar with the conditions. If maps and predictions about climatic changes are available, surely one ought to consult them. Each bit of knowledge made possible by astronomical, geological and geographical studies thus serves as a foundation for ethics as a science to the extent that it provides understanding of some of the conditions present in ethical situations.

BIOLOGICAL SCIENCES

Biology, the science of life, has discovered the chemical constituents and processes of protoplasm, the nature of cells and how they divide, through a division of nuclear chromosomes determining hereditary characteristics. Despite thousands of different kinds of plants, animals and single-celled beings, all are alike in being made of protoplasm and in surviving and growing through cell division. Since protoplasm always contains twelve chemical elements—carbon, oxygen, nitrogen, hydrogen, sulphur,, calcium, magnesium, sodium, potassium, phosphorus, chlorine and iron—all living beings and, consequently, all ethical situations are alike in having all of these chemicals present, as well as protoplasm and cells, and the internal and environmental processes necessary for their survival. For example, food, including proteins, carbohydrates, fats, vitamins and water, are needed. Food must be digested and distributed, and wastes must be excreted. Each of these conditions necessary to life is present alike in all ethical situations; and the laws which pertain to maintaining them thus function as bases for conditional oughts relative to every ethical situation.

Botany, the science of plant life, has revealed how chlorophyll contributing to photosynthesis enables plants to manufacture organic foods out of inorganic materials, how different kinds of plants flourish in various kinds of soils, how to grow plants for food, which plants are poisonous, how to increase the nutritiousness of crops. A whole science of agriculture aids in providing and improving the world's food supply, whether directly from vegetables, fruits and grains or through use of these for raising animals. Since human beings have not yet learned to live from synthetic foods entirely, human life continues to depend upon plants, directly or indirectly, and so such dependence is itself a condition of every ethical situation. Many, if no longer most, of our ethical problems center about problems relating to the growing, distribution, manufacture, sale, ownership, preparation, control and consumption of foods. So botany as a science provides understanding of many laws of plant natures which function as bases for conditional oughts whenever they become relevant to ethical situations.

Zoology, the study of animal life in all its forms—many of which are useful and many of which are harmful to men, directly or indirectly—provides understanding both of the multifarious kinds of animals, each having its own nature and laws, and of those conditions common to and necessary to the existence, survival and health of all animals, including man. Knowledge about the dangerousness of diseases, insects, poisonous snakes and lions provides us with bases for conditional oughts, or ought nots, when these are encountered; and knowledge about domesticated animals—such as cows and chickens which provide milk and eggs for food, horses and water buffalo which are useful for riding or hauling, and dogs and cats which make good companions—provides us with bases for other conditional oughts or ought nots. The likenesses of some other animals to men causes many people to regard them as also having intrinsic value, and so they believe that killing, eating or harming them is immoral.

Physiology, or specifically human physiology, is a science or a complex set of sciences concerned with the skeletal, muscular, digestive, circulatory, respiratory, glandular, nervous, reproductive and other systems constituting the living body, together with the processes involved in their growth, development, healthy maintenance and decay, and with consequences of variations, normal or abnormal, in conditions affecting health, such as diseases, malnutrition, toxication, poisonous foods or air, extremes of temperature or pressure, and lack of exercise. Every principle concerning essential conditions of human life and health discovered by physiologists constitutes a uniformity present in all ethical situations where life and health are at stake. Each may serve as a basis for conditional oughts whenever one becomes aware of its relevance.

Complexities are so great that physicians find it necessary to become more and more specialized in their studies and skills in order to serve with greater assurance. Hence, not only are there universal conditions of life in general but also universal conditions relative to more specific processes such as tooth decay, pregnancy, broken bones and allergies, which serve as bases for more specific conditional oughts. Textbooks on physiology are not textbooks on ethics; but each known physiological principle is such that one ought to take it into account in any situation where decisions and actions based on it are believed likely to produce better or worse results. Health manuals often include lists of rules stated in terms of oughts. But such oughts, whether stated conditionally or unconditionally, usually are intended as conditional oughts; e.g. the command, "Get eight hours sleep every night," means that other things being equal, if you are an average person of a certain age and wish to maintain optimum health, then you ought to try to attain approximately eight hours or restful sleep every night. But such oughts are conditional, not actual. Knowledge of such conditional oughts may contribute to an actual ought, as when one says, "I'm far behind in my sleep, so I must get to bed early tonight."

PSYCHOLOGICAL AND EPISTEMOLOGICAL SCIENCES

Grouping together and summarizing some of the sciences that are popularly called "mental," we single out for consideration those areas of investigation called psychology, epistemology, logic and mathematics, philosophy of science, and philosophy of language.

Psychology is a science which investigates the nature of awareness, consciousness, sensation, perception, conception, memory, imagination, feeling, emotion, volition, learning, habit, attitude, adaptability, inference and self-ideas, and the kinds of causes producing variations in their patterns of growth and manifestation. If, as I suspect, all of the foregoing in some way or other are necessary conditions of ordinary experience, they are also necessary conditions of ethical experience. If so, then all of the principles about uniformities discovered relative to them are also uniformities present in all ethical situations. Universal psychological laws (i.e. those serving necessary conditions of experience) are preconditions for ethical laws in the sense that no ethical experiences can occur without them. To whatever extent a psychological law functions significantly in any ethical situation, awareness of it as a basis for a conditional ought may be a decisive factor in determining a particular choice and thus causing a particular actual ought. It is not the function of either psychology or ethics as sciences to assert actual oughts; but since actual oughts always involve awareness of feelings of obligations about goals of action conceived in particular ways, the more one understands psychology (including social psychology, treated below) the greater the number of psychological factors which serve as bases for conditional oughts which can be taken into consideration in facing particular decisions.

Epistemology, the science inquiring into the nature of knowledge, truth and certainty, explores problems related to objects and subjects, appearance and reality, truth and error, belief and doubt, certainty and uncertainty, intuition and inference, and their relations to each other and to other psychological, physiological and physical conditions of knowing. Since ethical knowledge is knowledge, all of the essentials, i.e. universal, conditions of knowledge are also essential conditions of ethical knowledge. Hence, every uniformity discovered by epistemologists as essential to knowledge serves as a uniformity in all ethical situations, unless, perhaps, there can somehow be ethical situations without knowledge.

Since, as will be shown in a later chapter, inferences about the existence and nature of values often are erroneous because judgers are inexperienced or incautious about keeping epistemological distinctions in mind, many errors attributed to ethical judgments are basically epistemological in nature. To the extent that this is so, the conclusions of epistemologists not only may serve as bases for conditional oughts but also may be used to avoid errors in judgment which aggravate ethical predicaments. Unfortunately, to the extent that any scientist, including epistemologists, has failed to discover or ascertain uniformities which actually exist, others, such as ethical scientists, who depend upon him for such discoveries or ascertainments may suffer inadequacy as a result.

Logic and mathematics, sciences of structure abstractedly conceived, are designed to reveal the formal features of structures wherever they occur. As such, their concern is primarily with uniformities, whether conceived in terms of "classes," or "propositions" and "sets of propositions," and "relations." They are concerned with clarity, definiteness, definition; with the "truth" and "falsity" of propositions; with inferences, inductive and deductive; and with the "validity" and "invalidity" of inferences. Ignoring here controversies as to which kind of logic is most adequate—e.g. Aristotelian, traditional, symbolic, dialectical, inductive, pragmatic, Jain (*syadvada*), Buddhist, Chinese (*I Ching*) or organic—we note merely that, to whatever extent any abstract logic adequately represents minimal uniformities in all actual experiences or situations, it thereby represents minimal uniformities in all ethical experiences or situations.

For example, if a proposition cannot be both true and false in the same sense at the same time, then this "cannot," this impossibility, is uniformly an impossibility in all ethical situations. That is, all ethical situations are alike in that whatever is impossible anywhere is impossible in them. All such impossibilities constitute bases for conditional oughts. For example, if one seeks something actual, then he ought not to try to do the impossible. So, when a person discovers that a desired result is impossible to attain, then this discovery tends to be a determining factor in constituting an actual ought not.

Philosophy of science, the science which investigates the nature of science, does not pertain directly to uniformities common to all situations, for not all situations are properly called "scientific." Yet, indirectly, to the extent that there are certain conditions essential to, and thus common to, all sciences (e.g. scientific attitude, scientific method), they may have a bearing upon the relevance which all of the sciences we are here discussing have for ethical situations. Ignoring here the wide diversity of hypotheses about the nature of science still being entertained by philosophers of science, we suggest that certain minimums of attitude—such as willingness to remain open minded—and of method—such as stating conclusions as tentative hypotheses—affect the intended reliability of conclusions. That is, if in any ethical situation one appeals to a principle as "scientific," his failure to remember, or to know, that "scientific" means "tentative," he may mistake as "proved conclusively" conclusions which are not so intended. One may unwittingly depend too much, as well as too little, upon "science" as his authority. To the extent that certain kinds of ethical situations recur (e.g. those pertaining to deceit, theft, murder, taxation), if one believes that conclusions based upon scientific investigation are more reliable than those which lack investigation by scientific methods, then he believes a conditional ought. Recognition of a conditional obligation to try to be scientific relative to a particular kind of problem may well be a determining factor in causing an actual ought in someone, or many, to put forth the effort needed.

Philosophy of language, although a concern of peoples from earliest times, has received great attention recently, partly because the number and complexity of ways in which language is used have multiplied difficulties in understanding. Another reason for its interest is because many impatient professions, baffled by the intricacy of major philosophical problems and misled into accepting inadequate theories of knowledge, logic, reality and values, have, whether unwittingly or deliberately, found ways to excuse their failures by adopting philosophies of language which imply that many common and crucial words needed in stating them are meaningless and that, therefore, the problems themselves either are unsolvable or are "pseudo-problems."

Knowledge explosion has required distinguishing more meanings; uses for old words appear to have multiplied faster than invention of new words. Not only does enrichment of common usages increase possible ambiguities of words used in ordinary discourse, but, as is too often forgotten, each time a word is used in a slightly new context it tends to acquire a slightly new meaning. Increasing the number of ways in which even one person may use a word, such as "good," or "true," for example, as a result of becoming acquainted with its varying meanings in different areas of his life, by each of many specialists, in different historical and contemporary cultures, in different schools of philosophy, by different authors, as well as in different contexts, may make him increasingly uncertain as to what is meant when it is used in a next, somewhat new, context.

The importance of linguistic difficulties is belabored here as a reminder of additional kinds of factors conditioning all ethical situations, unless perhaps there are some situations in which we feel compelled to act even when we are unable to understand, or to linguify, the issues. If there are essential characteristics of language, or of the use of words as signs or symbols, of the sort explored in semiotics, semantics, syntactics, as well as linguistics, then these constitute ways in which all ethical situations involving language are alike. Although each such characteristic merely serves as a basis for a conditional ought (e.g. if I am uncertain about what the word "bad" signifies in this context, then I ought not assume that I am certain about the meaning which happens to occur to me), my awareness of uncertainty as a result of acquaintance with ambiguities due to complexities in language structure and with difficulties in communicating clearly between two different minds may be the decisive factor in an actual situation causing me to feel that I actually ought to refrain from retorting when my well-intended act has been condemned as "bad."

SOCIAL SCIENCES

Although "social science" refers to scientific investigations of all situations in which two or more persons interact, we shall limit our survey to social psychology, sociology, political science and economics.

It may be, as I believe it is, the case that some ethical situations are such that only personal factors are significantly at stake in making decisions, and hence that, to this extent, any ways in which social situations are alike are irrelevant, nevertheless, persons are essentially social in their nature and not only do most of one's ethical concerns involve other people but also those which appear to be purely personal, because they involve satisfactions or frustrations which leave subtle effects upon the whole personality, may be seen to involve social aspects if we care to explore such indirect involvement far enough. In the following, I shall assume that persons are essentially social, and thus remarks about universals common to all social situations being therefore common to all ethical situations should be interpreted in light of the reservations needed in making this assumption.

Social psychology is of two sorts, the first focusing upon how the individual learns to adapt to and associate with another person, the second emphasizing the attitudes and behavior of individuals functioning as members of a group.

Our first sort presupposes all of the essentials previously discussed under "psychology" and expands its investigation by looking for factors in common to all situations where two people meet, interact, adapt and develop, either harmoniously or antagonistically. Genetic psychology, concerned first with a child-mother relationship and tracing successive steps in growth to maturity by adding other normal or abnormal relationships, may best reveal how and why certain essential conditions occur.

1. Whether self-ideas emerge in an infant prior to association, as is commonly supposed, or whether they result from his being treated as an object by others and discovering himself by ways in which he responds to such treatment, as George Herbert Mead claims, self-ideas do emerge and are conditioned by the way a person finds himself behaving.

2. Each of two persons must be aware that the other exists, and that he is not alone.

3. Each must develop attitudes toward the other, and become

aware that the other has attitudes toward him. Such attitudes include liking or disliking, more or less, which function as approving or disapproving and as esteeming or disesteeming.

4. If and as interaction continues, each responds in some way, thereby reciprocating, whether equally or unequally, and discovering ways of reciprocating.

5. Repeated reciprocation provides experience with a principle of reciprocation, i.e. the tendency to treat others as we are treated, both negatively and positively, giving rise to attitudes of fairness and unfairness, with their additional judgments of approval and disapproval. Such experiences contribute to habits of trust and distrust and knowledge of limitations on capacities for cooperation.

6. Implicit in such reciprocation, and in the valuative (appreciating through sympathetic insight) and evaluative (judging how much the other can be used again) attitudes which emerge, is the ends-means problem which persists, even if indistinctly.

Surely all of the foregoing six characteristics at least can be found as common to all genetic and other person-to-person, psychological situations, and thus to all person-to-person ethical situations.

Our second sort involves feelings of identity of an individual with his group. Such feelings range from those of complete identification of self with group, as in some tribal societies, to complete rejection of the group as inimical, with multitudes of variations as people participate in larger numbers of and more kinds of groups. Endurance of interaction with other members of a group, especially of primary or intimate groups in which one's well-being is cared for, promotes not only a sense of belonging but also of the value, the power and the unitive reality of the group. Although the nature of such reality, power and value may remain as mysterious as that of the self and other forces in the environment, feelings of sharing both ownership of and responsibility for such group tend to emerge, together with notions of distributive justice and other problems of individual-group relations.

All of the principles discovered by social psychologists as inherent in person-person and person-group relations can function as bases for conditional oughts which may be found useful in all relevant ethical situations. As participation in larger numbers of and more kinds of groups reveals great variations in the kinds of uniformities which prevail, one tends to find the uniformities which are limited to, and thus relative to, each particular group more significant for adaptive purposes than the more universal (common to all groups) uniformities which then tend to recede into the background of his consciousness. Such more universal uniformites nevertheless do continue to exist. Consequently, social growth in each individual increases his awareness of the relativity of so many conditional oughts. Healthy personalities accept each new kind of uniformity as an additional utility; but unfortunately, awareness of such relativity leads hasty generalizers to infer that all uniformities are relative and that no universal uniformities exist. The existence of conditional oughts relative only to particular kinds of situations in no way eliminates the existence of conditional oughts which have their basis in uniformities common to all social psychological situations. No area in the social sciences is more important for understanding ethics as a science than social psychology.

Sociology, which presupposes social psychology and serves as the most general of the social sciences, focuses its investigations upon the nature and kinds of groups; the processes of group development, conflict and accommodation, and decay; and the principles for structuring and perpetuating groups, which are called customs, mores, institutions and laws. Anthropology and history, which cannot receive separate treatment in this brief summary, explore primitive and long-range group phenomena with emphases upon thoroughness in the study of particular groups and eras.

If the reader will consult the contents of a standard textbook in sociology, he can discover the many kinds of questions raised. We cannot here presume that all such questions are settled, but only that if and when settled we should find, relative to each, one or more bases for conditional oughts (or ought nots, e.g. one ought not assume as universal something demonstrated to be not universal). We select only three kinds of questions pertaining to (1) mores and culture, (2) cultural lag and (3) special-purpose groups.

1. People in groups, especially all-purpose groups—such as families, tribes, villages, states and nations—develop common

behavior patterns in all of several areas. All involve language; methods of acquiring food; family relationships; tools; clothing and shelter; systems of ownership, control and division of labor or responsibility; and means of protection, educating the young, treating disease and disposing of the dead. Although research continues relative to essentials of a universal cultural pattern, we know already that all such essentials provide uniformities which a science of ethics must take into consideration.

The extent to which individual conformity to common patterns is required varies, but principles of such variation are to be found in sociological distinctions between folkways, mores and laws, or those which can be deviated from without penalty, with opinion-enforced penalty, and officially enforced penalties, respectively. In general, the more dangerous a group regards deviation from the pattern, the greater the penalty and the stricter the enforcement. Hence group mores constitute large areas of conditional oughts for individuals, since, when the detection and enforcement are effective, an individual's knowledge of the mores and of the consequences of violation condition his conscience as established kinds of obligation.

Although mores function merely as conditional oughts (i.e. if a person is faced with conforming or not conforming to a particular law, then he will have to decide actually what he ought to do), the facing of some such decisions—such as sharing food, settlement of disputes and disposal of the dead—is almost inevitable. The more vital a conformity is deemed essential to welfare, the more emphatic teachers are likely to be; hence recipients of moral instruction often learn to fear the consequences of violation as if they were, somehow, ever-present actual oughts. The inability of impatient teachers to explain the multiplicities of complex alternatives as conditional oughts, and the fact that most moral training occurs in childhood before understanding of complexities and conditionalities is possible, cause most people to learn about mores as urgent commands and dogmatic demands. An infant in danger hears a shout or scream from his mother, "Stop!" "Don't do that!" He often learns "don't" and "spank" without learning why.

When the demandingness of requests for moral conformity exceeds understanding of the reasons for, i.e. benefits of, conformity, it appears as an evil to be avoided if possible. When a learner discovers that the demands are actually unjustified, he loses respect for the demander and the demands. Loss of confidence in moral advisers, and associating duties, obligations and oughts with negative commands, miseducates most people who then fail to recognize them as basically positive and as originating in self-interest and as probably self-evidently justified when one knows the reasons for them. Adults often observe with amusement how a disobedient child becomes the mother of equally disobedient children, and that the advice rejected by the child automatically becomes obviously needed when the child becomes a more-knowing and caring mother.

Unfortunately, a screaming mother's demand is an actual ought. And when she says "Never do that again!" the intended universality, or "absoluteness," of the command usually neglects and beclouds the fact that the postive basis of the command is a conditional ought, namely, "If faced with a similar situation in which your well-being is jeopardized, then for reasons which, although not clear to you now, you would, if you understood them, accept as obvious, and thus the course of action commanded as best for you and as what you really want."

The origin of mores is no mystery. The care which some people have for others, especially which parents have for children, causes them to teach those ways of behaving which they have found to be good or best; such teaching, when learned, constitutes the creation of cutlure. And culture consists in transmitted conditional oughts, together with the artifacts found useful in connection with them.

2. Cultural lag consists in teaching, learning and practicing beliefs about conditional oughts which, even though they were adequately adapted to past types of situations, are no longer adequate for present kinds of situations. Beliefs about the best ways of behaving become habits. Habits are hard to change. Group habits, mores, are said to be institutionalized. When institutions compel conformity after the need for them has disappeared, they become "formalistic." The naturalness of cultural lag, and of the typical difficulties and evils resulting from it, has been generalized upon by sociologists

in terms of a "Cycle of Institutional Development,"* and depicted as having the following typical stages:

(a) "Incipient organization," when a group responds to a felt need by adopting a common behavior pattern believed beneficial for meeting the need. (b) "Efficiency," when conformity to the behavior pattern does meet the need and participants understand and recognize the benefits and feel such conformity as freeing them from the recognized evils. (c) "Formalism," when conformity is felt as obligatory even though such conformity no longer provides benefits; when claimed benefits are no longer realized, forced conformity is experienced as evil. (d) "Disorganization," when some do and some do not conform; those who do not, regard those who do as foolish; whereas those who do, regard those who do not as immoral. Such disagreement results in mutual distrust, loss of moral guidance, demoralization, lack of group loyalty and growth in self-ishness. The evils of group demoralization themselves then generate needs for overcoming them by group decision.

(e) "Disintegration" occurs when old mores cease to function as felt obligations. It may be caused by failure of new members to assent to useless mores, or it may be caused by group decision to discontinue conformity. (f) If the need which the institution served continues (e.g. need for regulating sharing of food, settling disputes and disposal of the dead; or all those which all groups face inevitably), then some new commonly accepted behavior pattern needs to be devised. Sometimes the old institution is revised; then moral change is revolutionary. But, if the new institution is not well adapted, or if the penalties for nonconformity are either too lax or too severe, repetition of the evils apparent in the Cycle of Institutional Development will be hastened. Groups are said to be intelligent when they keep their institutions in the stage of efficiency, deliberately repealing laws as they become formalistic, even enacting laws with automatic expiration dates when expected changes cause doubts about their enduring value.

Not only do individuals and groups discover useful principles for group cooperation which serve as conditional oughts, but now that

---

*See Cooley, Angel, and Carr, *Introductory Sociology* (New York, Charles Scribner's Sons, 1933), pp. 406-414.

sociologists have discovered the evils as well as benefits resulting from institutions passing through the Cycle of Institutional Development, active attention to use of intelligence in keeping mores efficient also becomes an important conditional ought. That is, if and when an institution ceases to be efficient, then persons responsible for group decisions ought to give attention to its revitalization. The increasing interdependence of not only persons but also of their institutions as life becomes more megalopolitan both makes modification more difficult, more expensive to accomplish, and more subject to disruptive influences, on the one hand, and makes delay in dealing with the evils of cultural lag even more crucial because the cost of demoralization and of cataclysmic changes forced by revolution are much greater. Is not failure to apply scientific methods in this area, i.e. to develop ethics as a science and consequent faith in informed ethical engineering, itself one of our major conditional oughts being habitually overlooked today?

3. The obvious values of special-purpose groups, resulting from division of labor and increasing skill and efficiency in serving such purposes, function as conditional oughts whenever we discover a new purpose or a new and better way of serving such a purpose through a new group. But also the evils resulting from increasing competition between such groups, especially when their officers develop vested interets and they develop cultural lag, from tendencies toward tyrannical decisions by such officers, and from the increasing impersonality with which such decisions are made and the effects received by persons, are becoming well known. If the needs of persons are met more and more through services by special-purpose groups, and if this decreases the ratio of average participation by persons in primary groups, where persons associate more intimately as whole persons in ways where their own intrinsic values are respected and promoted, then the problems resulting from depersonalization and dehumanization increase in importance. Conditional oughts relative to the optimum percentages of participation in personal versus impersonal association, and to their variations under differing conditions, assume greater significance as society speeds up its quest for appropriating the values of rapidly multiplying special-purpose groups.

The foregoing sample of issues dealt with by sociologists insufficiently suggests not only the multitudes of ways in which social, and hence ethical, situations are the same but also the multi-multitudes of additional different areas, including many very new areas in which uniformities serving as bases for conditional oughts exist.

Political science pertains to social control and to the needs people in groups have for controlling and being controlled. As groups vary in size, governments may vary in complexity, from family, village, township, country, state, region, nation and world, and in numbers and kinds of functions which they perform. Speaking of any and all such governments as "the state," we find it involving at least four essential elements—people, territory, sovereignty and system of government. Insofar as ethical situations are political in nature, they too are alike in having all four such essentials.

Political groups all need performance of legislative, administrative and judicial functions, and involve some definite location and distribution of authority for each of these functions. Legislation determines policy decisions which become established as "laws." Violation of a law is a "crime." "Civil law" pertains to established "rights," "privileges" and "duties" of citizens. Problems of justice and injustice—distributive and retributive—between citizens, between individuals and groups and between groups normally occur and the need for dealing with them requires officers, elected or appointed, whose responsibilities are defined. Since, in general, the aim of group control is group welfare, all political issues are also ethical issues, and all political decisions are ethical decisions. Hence, ethics as a science is concerned not only with ways in which all ethical situations are alike, which may be called "general ethics," but also with all of the kinds of situations—political, economic, educational, religious, etc.—in which obligations occur, which may be called "special ethics," or more specifically, "political ethics," "economic ethics," "educational ethics," "religious ethics," etc. Such specific ethics may also be "scientific" in the sense that they too can deal with ways in which all situations of their specific kind or kinds are alike and yield principles which can function as bases for conditional oughts.

Group welfare normally involves need for protecting the security of the state from external aggression, and thus for political adaptation to such needs, including military preparedness at times, as well as the internal security from whatever disruptive or debilitating evils may occur. Aging of citizens and officers, and changes in resources, abilities and interests, create needs for shifts in the focus of power and authority, often causing strain on the relations between citizens. As resources increase or decrease in abundance, ideas about minimums of welfare for citizens may change, affecting ideas of, and the feasibility of trying to maintain, various "freedoms" as rights.

Regardless of how various and complicated are the kinds of political situations involving decisions about welfare, all such situations are, invariably, ethical in the sense that someone is faced with an issue requiring choice among alternative values and thereby creating obligations relative to such choice. Growth of reliable knowledge about the nature of government, both general and specific, i.e. advancement in the achievement of political science as a science, is an aid in providing additional knowledge about relevant conditional oughts, and thus serves also as growth in ethics as a science.

Economics studies the production, distribution, exchange and consumption of goods and services which are in demand but limited in supply. "Goods and services" are things or activities which can satisfy "wants," whether needs or desires, which are called "demands." Such "goods and services" are said to have "utility" or usefulness, and thus function as instrumental values. (See Chapter 3 for treatment of relations between instrumental and intrinsic values.) Hence, economics, like political science which is concerned with public welfare, is basically a value science.

Although obviously not all ethical situations are economic in nature, many of them deal primarily with economic problems and many more have economic conditions functioning in them, either directly (as when a person fails to keep a promised recreational appointment because required to work overtime) or indirectly (because few persons can exist for long apart from groups depending on economic conditions which thus function as conditions of his own personality as he enters each new ethical situation). In this sense, all ethical situations are alike insofar as economic principles are essential to the operation of the society in which the person, as ethical, exists. Thus all economic principles serve as bases for conditional oughts to whatever extent economic factors are known to be present in an actual decision situation.

On the other hand, all economic problems, both theoretical and practical, calling for decision or choice among alternatives are also, thereby, ethical problems. A review of the kinds of problems which occur in each of the areas of economics may serve also as a review of kinds of ethical problems. For, in the area of production, issues about production of goods—such as relative cost of production, efficiency, overproduction, waste, employment of labor versus automation, exhaustion of limited resources, disposal of waste products, division of labor—all present themselves as ethical because they call for decisions among values. Increase in productivity for needed goods is important to individuals, to groups, to industries, to nations (referred to as the Gross National Product) and to mankind.

In the area of distribution, transportation of products from producer to consumer may be direct, as when a farmer eats his own apples, or indirect, as when he sells them at a local market to a wholesaler who ships them to a warehouse for storage before reselling to a buyer for a grocery chain who has them shipped to the chain warehouse before going to the particular store where some are purchased by the cook in the local pastry shop for baking into pies to be sold to a restaurant for resale to customers. Each step in such a process tends to involve ethical decisions relative to costs, efficiency, labor, deterioration and misadjustments about demands. Distribution of shares of the goods produced according to the factors of production, such as costs of raw materials and tools, wages for labor, interest for capital, rent for land or buildings, insurance, profits for management, "unearned increments," taxes for public services, etc., all require judgments as to the best way of proceeding, thereby constituting ethical problems.

In the area of exchange, exchange of ownership of goods presupposes principles of ownership; methods of exchange (such as goods for goods versus goods for money, barter versus fixed price, immediate versus credit payment); fair price; honesty in representing goods, ownership, credit, etc.; and reliability regarding keeping agreements. Introduction of money as a means for facilitating exchange, credit, accounting and storage of capital brings with it hosts of ethical issues relative to the soundness of money due to inflationary and deflationary tendencies; problems of international exchange of currency; detection and prevention of counterfeiting; ease of theft, establishment of banks, control of banks, supervision of banking practices, credit ratings, bankruptcy, loans, interest rates, etc. Hosts of ethical problems recur relative to each. Discovery of principles relative to ownership, exchange, money, price, banking and credits, both those in economics as a "pure" science and those in the applied sciences of business and public administration, provides us with additional quantities of bases for conditional oughts.

In the area of consumption, problems of waste, poverty, minimum and ideal standards of living, population explosion increasing demand above supply, over-stimulation of desires by advertising, "truth in advertising," "truth in packaging," etc., are filled with ethical issues. Needs for mass consumption of products in order to make use of mass products in order to make use of mass production of products feasible, and shifts from an "economy of scarity" to an "economy of abundance" in some sections, and for aid to people in developing countries while the gap between the haves and have-nots increases, and other shifts in economic conditions, such as from prosperity to depression or vice versa, create special problems.

Concluding our sketch of the social sciences, we repeat the claim that genuine advancement in knowledge of the principles operating in each field constitutes advancement in ethics as a science to the extent that such principles become available as factors conditioning choices. This claim holds for both those universals common to all social situations and those common to each of the kinds of social situations.

AXIOLOGICAL SCIENCES

Since ways in which all value situations are alike will be the focus of special attention in Chapters 3, 4 and 5, we defer discussions of the evidence until then. We will distinguish axiology, or the general science of value, from aesthetics and philosophy of religion as well as from ethics. Understanding of universals discoverable within each of these fields as well as those pertaining to all value situations is essential to a complete understanding of ethics as a science.

ETHICAL SCIENCES

Although all ethical situations are value situations, not all value situations are ethical, as we shall see. A proposal regarding the nature of ethics, and hence regarding what constitutes the specifically ethical component common to all ethical situations, will be made in Chapter 6. Convenience dictates distinguishing those problems and principles common to all ethical situations which a person faces as an individual, regardless of whether other persons are intentionally involved, which may be called "individual ethics," from those common to ethical situations where a person functions as a member of a group and where the welfare of the group is at stake, which may be called "social ethics." We devote two chapters, 8 and 9, to these areas respectively.

PART II
VALUES

CHAPTER 3

INTRINSIC VALUES

A LTHOUGH ON THE SURFACE the field of values appears to be in
utter confusion, sufficiently painstaking analysis of factors
in value situations can lead to clear understanding. Too many
people are too hasty in their judgments, too impatient for results,
too quick to give up when initial hypotheses fail. Should one
expect and insist that inquiry into the nature of values will yield
less complicated solutions than inquiries into the nature of physical
energy? The hypothesis proposed here, although complex, is relatively simple in its general outlines when compared with many
physical hypotheses. Yet it is one which every person can test for
himself whenever he chooses. It involves subhypotheses about
intrinsic values, objectified values (see Chapter 4) and potential
values (see Chapter 5).

MEANS VERSUS ENDS

Essential to clarity in value theory is the common distinction
between means and ends, technically called "instrumental values"
and "intrinsic values." A "means value" or "instrumental value"
is any value which depends for its existence as a value upon its
serving as a means to the bringing into existence or maintaining
in existence an intrinsic value. And "end value" or "intrinsic
value" is a value which is self-contained in the sense that it is not
required to serve any other value in order for it to be a value.
For example, if you are enjoying tasting a sweet flavor, not because it causes you to want more (which it may also do), but
just because you find the sweet flavor enjoyable as a sweet flavor,
such enjoyment exemplifies intrinsic value. Now if you could not
have enjoyed that sweet flavor unless you had first put a particular

piece of candy in your mouth, then that particular piece of candy is not only an instrumental value or means to your enjoyment but also a necessary one.

Troubles arise because we habitually identify intrinsic value with instrumental value or, rather, fail to distinguish between them. If you say, "I like that sweet candy," you are locating the sweetness occurring in your mouth as if it were in its apparent cause, namely, the piece of candy. And if you do not distinguish between the sweetness and your enjoyment of it, then you tend to project the enjoyment itself as if it were in the candy. If you then take the piece of candy out of your mouth, as children do with suckers, and look at it, you may then say, "That's good candy," thereby judging that the candy itself is good because it is enjoyable. It is good, instrumentally, when it causes enjoyment. But the enjoyment, the intrinsic value, is not in the candy. Further difficulties involved in such experiences will be examined in the following two chapters. The point being made thus far is that the failure to keep in mind the distinction between intrinsic and instrumental values is fatal to clarity. It is a fundamental part of my hypothesis that without discovering and keeping in mind a clear distinction between intrinsic and instrumental values, a sound science of values is impossible.

FOUR KINDS OF INTRINSIC VALUES

At least four distinguishable kinds of intrinsic value which can be enjoyed by everyone have been recognized by theorists for centuries if not millenia. My hypothesis is not new in the sense that it introduces new kinds of intrinsic value, but it is new, so far as I know, in the sense that it recognizes all four and condemns those theories which limit recognized intrinsic value to only one, two or even three of them. Let me first examine each of these four kinds by stating theories claiming each to be the most basic if not the only kind of intrinsic value.

Pleasant Feeling

The view that intrinsic good consists in pleasant feeling and intrinsic evil consists in unpleasant feeling, especially pain, is one of the oldest, having been called "Hedonism" since ancient Greek times. Pleasant feelings are experienced most obviously in particular sensory enjoyments such as sweet flavors; fragrant odors; brilliant colors; dulcet tones; smooth, soft and warm feelings; and even tickling sensations. Unpleasant feelings likewise are experienced not only in pains and aches but also in nausea; sour or bitter flavors; foul odors; drab or discordant colors; screeching sounds; extremely hard, rough, hot or cold feelings; and in dizziness.

After Hedonism was condemned as a "pig philosophy," since animals also experience many such feelings, more attention was given to subtler pleasures such as those enjoyed in agreeable conversation, reading poetry, hearing symphonic music, and even "pleasures of the intellect" such as those enjoyed in philsophical argumentation or in facile mathematical calculation. These were said to be "higher quality" pleasures. Yet the persistent acceptance of sensory models as the most obvious kinds of intrinsic values is reflected in attempts at qualitative descriptions of high-level displeasures such as a "sour note" in music, a "bitter argument" or a "foul play."

Satisfaction of Desire

Intrinsic value consists in the feeling of satisfaction and intrinsic evil in feeling frustrated. This view, also one of the oldest, being expounded early in India, locates the source of both good and evil in desire, wanting or willing, and hence may be called "Voluntarism." Without desire there can be neither satisfaction nor frustration, neither good nor evil. Although desires vary in intensity from merest whim to insistent demand, everyone may observe enjoying satisfaction most simply when slaking his thirst or eating after prolonged hunger. Feelings of achievement, whether in acquiring through strenuous effort, attaining some ambitious goal, overcoming a threat to security or regaining a lost possession, exemplify the end quality of the means-end relationship. Frustration is experienced whenever one is prevented from obtaining what he wants, and occurs both in subtler forms, such as hopeless yearning, fear of insecurity and anxiety about prospects, and in more obvious forms, such as anger or a tantrum.

Enthusiasm

Not satisfaction of desire, but desirousness itself is the location of the greatest enjoyment according to Romanticism. While desiring, one is alive, vital, future-oriented, purposive, active, motivated. When satisfaction kills desire, one is dead, dormant, passive, inert. So enjoyment of intrinsic value occurs while one feels exuberant, eager, earnest, ardent, ambitious, willful, insistent, committed, convinced, passionate, excited, zestful, thrilled. Evil appears when interest wanes, exuberance disappears, hopelessness descends, vigor subsides. It is experienced as worst in complete apathy. Since frustration heightens one's interest, it is actually a form of good, especially when other kinds of desirousness have been sated. Hence, it is desiring, not satisfaction of desire, which is enjoyed as intrinsic value. It is better to have desire aroused, intensified and maintained insatiably than to have desire satisfied, quieted, terminated, according to Romanticism.

Contentment

When desire is experienced as wanting or lacking, the absence of what is wanted is felt as a deficiency, as a lack of what is good. Wanting, then, is experiencing incompleteness, imperfection, inadequacy, insufficiency. When one experiences deficiency, he idealizes completeness, fullness, wholeness, integrity. And he feels discontented, restless, anxious until he achieves rest, peace, quietude, contentment. Since desire is experienced as lacking intrinsic value, intrinsic value is idealized as experiencing lack of desire. Such lack of lack is felt as fullness, wholeness, as freedom from deficiency, as freedom from disturbance, as freedom from anxiety.

This view has been perfected in Hindu thought where *ananda,* bliss, is enjoyed as so completely faultless that even all traces of any desire for it has been forgotten. For convenience, we may thus call this view "Anandism." One may intuit for himself such contentment, purified of all desire, during moments when one is so utterly exhausted that he lacks energy enough to desire anything, when his bed feels so comfortable in the morning that he has no desire to get out of it, or when his stomach is so full after a festival banquet that it has "spoiled his appetitie." Yogins seek *nirvana* through trance, or "transcendental meditation," but some

Zen Buddhists seek *satori* as an ever-present aspect of everyday, busy experiences.

Once feelings of contentment have been enjoyed as intrinsic value, then one will try to avoid all that might disturb such contentment as intrinsic evil, especially desires and desirousness, but also pleasures as well as pains which arouse interest, and satisfactions which are felt as so good that one wants to seek more such satisfaction. Since life does not permit absence of these for long, one may then, practicing depth psychology, enjoy a deep-seated feeling of confidence of at-home-ness in the universe while relegating disturbing desires, satisfactions, frustrations, enthusiasms, pleasures and pains to surface phenomena. When one enjoys a profounder level of contentment, he can endure his surface-level troubles with considerable disinterest or detachment.

A NEW HYPOTHESIS

Building upon the four preceding theories, each long standing in human culture, one may conclude, simply, that all are true, or partly true, to the extent that each points to something which clearly exists in human experience. But such a conclusion involves holding that each is also false, i.e. partly false, to the extent that it claims that the kind of intrinsic value it points to is the only kind, or at least the only superior or supreme kind. The new hypothesis proposed here is that all four of the kinds of experiences—namely, feelings of pleasantness, satisfaction, enthusiasm and contentment—are enjoyed by all people at some time or other, and indeed much of the time in some degree as ends in themselves, either in their pure form, occasionally, or blended in varying ways; and that feelings of pain, frustration, apathy and lacking completeness are experienced by all people at some time or other in some degree as intrinsic evils.

This hypothesis does not claim that these four are the only kinds. I have been forced to change my view before, by assenting to evidence called to my attention by studies in Romantic literature and Hindu philosophy, and may be forced to do so again. But the four kinds now appear to me to constitute a well-integrated set, as evidence presented below will suggest. And together they appear sufficient, and sufficiently both clear and distinct on the one hand and sufficiently complementary on the other, to provide an adequate basis for launching further systematic scientific research regarding them as the foundational intrinsic values upon which all other kinds of values, not merely objectified and potential (see two following chapters), but also all instrumental values, economic values, political values, artistic values, religious values, and upon which all kinds of ethical obligations and consequent notions of duty, rightness and justice are based.

How New?

The novelty of the hypothesis does not consist in pointing to a new kind of intrinsic value, but in calling attention to the fact that all are needed for an adequate account of experience and of intrinsic value, and that, whether singly or in blends, function as the intrinsic value aspects of more complex gestalts. Many of the multifarious ways in which such gestalts occur do persist as distinguishable kinds of experiences; and one may, if he wishes, say that there are just that many kinds of intrinsic values. Behavioristically, the occurrence of such persistence is sufficient to observe and name the kind as a distinguishable kind of value. One may, if he wishes, claim novelty for this hypothesis as giving support to the view that there are many kinds of intrinsic value (and that many more will emerge as creativity continues), but whatever their complexities or their limitations, they are conditioned by the same factors causing feelings of pleasantness, satisfaction, enthusiasm and contentment to occur in the first place, and they could be analyzed, in principle, into aspects distinguishable in terms of our four basic types. In fact, in most ordinary experiences the four aspects intermingle and blend almost indistinguishably, and this is part of the reason why confusion persists in value theory as well as in personal value judgments.

Without taking time here to show how each of the four theories —Hedonism, Volutarism, Romanticism and Anandism—argues for its own superiority, we mention some differences between the four kinds of value before considering their similarities and how they supplement each other.

Differences

Pleasant and unpleasant feelings occur most obviously in pleasing and painful sensations, such as a sweet flavor or a skin prick. Typically, sensory pleasures and pains have spatial and temporal location and may occur without having been desired. Spatial location may be illustrated by sweet flavors being tasted in the mouth, fragrant odors in nostrils, bright colors in one's vision, and a painful cut in the skin of one's left thumb, for example. We do not locate color in the mouth, flavors in the nose, or odor in eyes. Sensations and sensuous pleasures and pains have beginning and ending, sometimes clearly defined, as when a finger is pricked and then a sliver is removed. Although some sensory experiences do occur because we desire to have them, such desiring is not essential to their nature. Colors, odors and pains often appear unexpectedly, as something presented to us and not as something desired. They may, on the other hand, cause us to desire to continue them, repeat them or remove them. Biologically we seem so constructed that sensations attract our attention and arouse desires for or against their continuation. In such cases at least, sensation and sensory pleasure and displeasure precede the desire which may lead (and in this sense precede) to further pleasure or displeasure.

Desires, on the other hand, although they too are temporal— having beginning, duration and termination—usually are much less clear, especially their termination. Although a desire may be aroused suddenly—as when a finger is pricked a desire to have the pain stop may begin immediately, and removal of the pricker may be accompanied by a feeling of satisfaction—experience often remains suffused with a lingering quality, due perhaps to the fact that one's whole self seems to be involved in this desiring. Desires seldom have a spatial location. When I desire, the "I" which desires is hard to locate spatially, except, of course, that it is inside my body. When I desire a specific object, the object may be spatially locatable; but that which does the desiring or is desiring or, more specifically, is the desire, may not occur as being any "where." Although other things may cause me to desire, it is I who does the desiring. In this sense, my desire is not experienced as something presented to me but as something arising out of my self. Hence, the intrinsic values occurring as sensory pleasures and those occurring as aspects of desire are different in nature.

But feelings of satisfaction or frustration, enthusiasm or apathy, and contentment or anxiety, although all desire-based, also differ from each other. Satisfaction is felt as termination of desire through achievement. Enthusiasm requires no termination and may be experienced as interminable or at least without thought of termination. Contentment requires termination of desire by its extinction, regardless of whether or not there has been achievement. Frustration normally intensifies desire. Apathy is experienced as absence of desire. Anxiety is annoyance with desire. Note that contentment, emphasized by Anandism as the supreme value, and apathy, emphasized by Romanticism as the supreme evil, both involve absence of desire. Enthusiasm emphasized by Romanticism as the supreme good, and anxiety emphasized by Anandism as the supreme evil both involve desirousness. Frustration, regarded as evil by Voluntarists, is often experienced as good by Romanticists; and satisfaction, regarded as good by Voluntarists, is often experienced as evil by Romanticists. Continuing feelings of satisfaction of desire, which thereby maintain awareness of the desire being satisfied (exemplified when one continues to be proud of his success), and feelings of satisfaction which serve as latent desires for more of the same, are regarded as good by Voluntarism but as evil by Anandism. Since without desire there can be no satisfaction, for Voluntarism, absence of desire is instrumentally evil, at least; but with desire there can be no contentment for Anandism, so the presence of desire is intrinsically evil. Hence, the three desire-based kinds of intrinsic value also differ essentially in nature.

Similarities

On the other hand, all four kinds of intrinsic value are basically alike in several respects: (a) All involve awareness and have no actual existence apart from such awareness. Each must be experienced in order to be actually. (b) All are directly intuited. Their existence, and their existence as intrinsic values, is self-evident because this is what they are experienced as. One may not attend to them as such, for he may and, as we shall point out below, normally does focus his attention upon objects, more or less conceptualized, in ways such that he attributes such value to them. So their presence in intuited gestalts may occur without clear awareness of them; this is especially true when our experiences are motivated rather than contemplative, for then the instrumental value aspects of objects as experienced tend to dominate. (c) All may be spoken of as "felt," and all intrinsic goods may be spoken of as being "enjoyed," and all intrinsic evils may be described as "suffering."

(d) All appear variably, or as more or less. That is, sensory pleasures may be more or less pleasant, satisfactions may be more or less satisfactory, enthusiasms may be more or less intense, and one may feel more or less contented. Sometimes we may be more conscious of evil variations, such as being more painful, more frustrating, more apathetic or more discontented. One may, metaphorically, describe such variations in terms of degrees, but since their differences usually are experienced as vague, introduction of any conceptual system of degrees is likely to distort them or presume them to be more precise than they are; no direct method of measurement seems possible.

(e) All appear to have evolved out of, and to continue to depend upon, biological and physiological natures. But here we go beyond what is self-evident and appeal to indirect evidence assembled by other scientists. Apparently those animals which were able to achieve satisfaction of specific desires, and to enjoy such satisfaction as intrinsic value, were more likely to survive, other things being equal. Specific kinds of desires with supporting satisfaction, such as those for eating, drinking and reproducing, contributed to survival. And feelings of pleasantness connected with particular kinds of sensory end organs aided in survival, as did abundance of energy providing desirousness and enthusiasm in tackling difficult survival problems. It may be that, as our abilities to measure physiological phenomena increase, we can discover closer correlations between degree variations in some physiological changes and variations in experienced intrinsic values. We may then develop greater control over increasing enjoyments, though whether we can "improve" our abilities to torture or otherwise cause people to suffer may be doubted. But we already have enough evidence from direct intuition of variations in intrinsic values to provide a sufficient basis for ethics as a behavioral science.

How Supplementary?

Our four kinds of intrinsic value not only are both different and alike in the ways pointed out above, but also supplement each other in constituting experience in several ways. We mention three.

1. The four kinds of intrinsic value interdepend in the sense that each needs the other to supply the remainder of the kinds of intrinsic value constituting experience. Recognition of all is needed for an adequate theory of value experience. Such interdependence will be illustrated by the following two ways and even more intricately in the next two chapters.

2. Each varies, not merely in the sense that there may be more or less of it, but also to the extent to which it constitutes a predominant kind of value in experience at any one time or over periods of time. Although each may occupy present experience with relatively complete dominance, so that one may be aware of only one, also all may be present together as aspects of a whole and in such ways that sometimes one and sometimes another may predominate.

One may, despite the latent associated biological mechanisms which arouse desire, be aware of, contemplate and enjoy sensory experiences without having a desire aroused either to continue or to repeat the awareness. On the other hand, when pleasant sensation occurs, normally a tendency exists for our bodily organism to become aroused, especially when the sensation becomes intense, and when one possesses sufficient energy with which to respond, and when other factors, including competing sensations, do not distract attention from it, and when one has not been conditioned negatively to resist arousal of such desire. Sensation and desire interdepend instrumentally in that sensation is required for the arousal of some desires and that full functioning, continuation and recurrence of some sensations and pleasant feelings depend upon arousing desire to attend to, continue and repeat them. Establishment of a habit to enjoy certain kinds of sensations serves to create or activate desires which will lead to their furtherance. Such additional occurrences depend for their existence in experience upon such desires.

Although desire may be aroused by sensation and sensation by desire, desire, including desirousness, may be aroused without significant awareness of sensation. Desire is related to and dependent upon the presence of sufficient energy. Sometimes energy production becomes superabundant and manifests itself spontaneously as desire for activity. Although one may not be able to act without involving some sensation, his awareness may be so fully occupied with his burgeoning desire as to exclude attention to sensation. Furthermore, one may have such surge of desire without having formulated conceptually anything that is desired. One may thus enjoy desiring without knowing what he desires or what it will take to satisfy it. Although in a developed person ideas of what one wants tend to stimulate desires, genetically the feeling of desire is prior to ideation about specific goals which will satisfy desire. Even adults sometimes become restless and want to do something without being sure what they want to do. Such restlessness may be felt as discomforting, but expansive bursts of energy may be enjoyed for themselves alone. If one did not enjoy desiring, he might never go on to seek satisfaction, especially when the course leading to some satisfactions is very arduous. Even though desire and satisfaction are linked together biologically, not only desire but even exuberance or desirousness are in a fundamental sense prior to satisfaction.

Nevertheless, perpetual exuberance leads to exhaustion. Desire, even when not aroused by specific sensory stimuli or the appearance of some problem needing solution, tends to formulate itself in terms of some objective or goal which will satisfy it. Without such goal, desire remains vague, inchoate, directionless. With such a goal, desire aims at it, and satisfaction is conceived in terms of attaining it. When the satisfaction settles what was aroused, a feeling of completion results. The feeling of satisfaction lasts so long as there remains any awareness of this settling of what was aroused.

As long as energy continues to produce desirousness, repeated feelings of satisfaction do not quiet desire. But when one feels that all of his desire has been satisfied, so that desire itself ceases to demand further attention, then he feels contented. Contentment is full culmination of desire and, just as satisfaction is felt as intrinsically good, so a feeling of contentment, or of full satisfaction, is felt as perfectly good.

Hence, our four intrinsic values interdepend through their depending for their existence and intensity upon interdepending biological mechanisms which appear to function causally the way they do because one or the other of the intrinsic value experiences tends to call for the others as natural consequences.

3. Intrinsic values appear to supplement each other successively, both in the production of particular kinds of complex value experiences and in predominating variably in different stages in a normal life cycle. Following are two supplemental hypotheses which, if accepted, tend to support the hypothesis that there are just four main kinds of intrinsic value and that they interdepend.

The first of these pertains to the distinguishable presence of all four in moderately rapid succession during normal sexual orgasm. Pleasant feelings accompanying the stimulation of erogenous zones often initiate desire, which then becomes aroused and grows in intensity to an impetuously passionate climax, which is followed by a feeling of intense satisfaction, and then subsides into a feeling of complete contentment in which even all of the previous experience tends to be forgotten.

The second claims that infants and children seem more often preoccupied with sensory pleasures and pains, and, though they often manifest violent exuberance, they seem more easily disturbed and pacified by sensuous means. Youth is a period of energy and enthusiasm; it is forward-looking, desirous, not easily satisfied with anything. Adulthood tends to be more occupied with attaining the goals of life and with recognizing that the goals are being attained; its concerns emphasize feelings of satisfaction. Old age, when both energy declines and the goals of life have been largely achieved, devotes itself more to feelings of contentment. Pleasures and pains, enthusiasm and apathy, satisfaction and frustration, and contentment and annoyance with anxiety occur at all ages and stages in life; but infancy, youth, adulthood and old age seem to be occupied somewhat more by each of the four, respectively.

HOW TEST?

1. DIRECT OBSERVATION. Each person can observe for himself whether or not the hypothesis holds for his own experiences. All

of the four kinds of intrinsic value are intuited. Nothing, surely, is more certain than the immediate data of one's own consciousness. Immediate apprehension of data is the starting point, or the empirical foundation, of all scientific evidence. And here each person has his own primary data to observe, so that he can be more certain of the evidence for this hypothesis than he can for those scientific theories for which apprehension is not directly available to him but only to specialists.

First, merely by reflection, one can recall many of his previous experiences under either varying or repeated circumstances regarding such values. Secondly, he can observe now with the sensory experiences he is having and with the desires he now has, unless his mind is so cluttered with preconceptions that he cannot focus upon such simple aspects of his experience or unless his sensations, desires and feelings are so weak as to appear neutral rather than as obviously enjoyed or suffered. Thirdly, he can deliberately experiment by planning to observe experiences in which the different kinds of values naturally occur. Fourthly, he can repeat his reflections, observations and experiments as many times as he feels needed to give the hypothesis a fair trial before reaching a tentative, but more tenacious, conclusion about it.

2. CONSULT OTHERS. A person discusses with others, especially those with whom one is intimately acquainted, so that he may feel more assured that communication about feelings is reliable. All direct evidence regarding feelings of enjoyment and suffering is private. But so is all direct evidence available to any scientist on any subject. One commonly recognized criterion of scientific reliability is that the problem, the hypothesis and the kind of data be communicable and that experiments can be repeated by others. That people can and do communicate about their feelings is obvious from the multitude of words which have come to be used for this purpose. It is obvious also to anyone who has to listen to complaints. But one may deliberately explore the issues raised by this hypothesis with others and probe his inquiry especially where he has doubts about it.

3. OBSERVE OTHERS. Although such evidence is indirect and involves inferences of many sorts, you may prefer to trust your more objective observations especially in areas where you feel sure

of your sympathetic insight. Those who watch infants and children constantly have plenty of opportunity to gather this kind of evidence. The same is true for those who care for the aged or the ill.

4. CONSULT LITERATURE. Here the resources are already vast. Works on sensation, emotion, feeling, will, desire and pleasure abound, ranging from earlier works in the histories of philosophy and psychology, including histories of aesthetics and ethics, to recent experiments by biologists, physiologists and physiological psychologists with the latest electronic devices. Much can be learned also from Hindu philosophical literature devoted to intricate analyses of introspective distinctions.

5. PROJECT RESEARCH. Although here most persons may have only limited opportunities, they may encourage, request and support research by others even when they cannot engage in such research themselves. Here I have in mind not only questionnaire types of investigation, sampling reports of people in various countries, cultures, classes, ages, etc., but also research in specific areas of value theory. Institutions interested in research, whether universities, foundations, scientific societies, government agencies or private corporations, are of many sorts. For example, all agencies concerned with human nature and its behavior—such as departments of education, military personnel, health, urban conditions, labor, psychology, psychiatry, religion, advertising, personnel management, pharmaceutical manufacturing, medicine, law, geriatrics, traffic safety, social science and humanities—all have an interest in the foundations of value theory and should be interested in promoting relevant research.

6. OBSERVE CONSEQUENCES. By this I mean observe how the hypothesis works in supporting theories in other areas, including ethical theory. One of the tests of a good theory is how well it fits with theories in other fields. A theory is hardly adequate if its explanations fail to cohere with accepted conclusions in other fields. This hypothesis should be examined relative to ways in which it provides additional support to working hypotheses in other value sciences such as economics, political science, aesthetics and philosophy of religion, as well as ethics. Such examination requires interest and ability in more than one field and competence in interdisciplinary comparisons. The following two chapters, with

their additional hypotheses about objectification of values and potential values, and the remainder of this volume, with its applications to problems in individual and social ethics, are designed to serve this purpose.

CHAPTER 4

VALUES AS OBJECTS

HOW ARE VALUES KNOWN?

INTRINSIC VALUES OCCURRING AS feelings of enjoyment or suffering are directly intuited. But so are the colors, shapes, sizes, relations and concepts of which we are aware. Yet, in ordinary experience, we experience them as objects of our attention, and, in doing so, we "objectify" them and often "reify" them. The technical distinction between "objectifying" and "reifying" is related to the well-known distinction between "apparent objects" and "real objects." How are values known? As apparent objects or as real objects?

The problem faced here is, how does it happen that, if intrinsic values exist as feelings within a person, they appear as if located in objects, and much of the time as if in real things? A thing is said to be "real" when it exists whether we are aware of it or not. The issues at stake here are primarily issues in theory of knowledge and secondarily issues in value theory and ethics. Knowledge of values is a kind of knowledge. So in inquiring into how values are known, we are plunged into the fundamental problems of the nature of knowledge, whether we like it or not.

I do not see how anyone can achieve clarity of understanding in either value theory or ethics until he has achieved clarity of understanding regarding the nature of knowledge. Hence, I believe that certain minimal insights into the nature of knowledge are essential for an adequate understanding of the nature of value and obligation. The problems of knowledge are notorious for their difficulty. But I believe the difficulties in theory of knowledge are due in large part to impatience and to hasty conclusions which often turn out to be unworkable. Many confusions occurring in ethical situations and in ethical theory are, or are a result of, confusions in theory of knowledge. Hence, failure to attend to, to penetrate and to master problems in theory of knowledge (and this is an indictment of our public school systems and our college and university systems) is in large part responsible for our failure to achieve understanding of, and a scientific treatment of, values and obligations. Our first task here is to explore some basic aspects of the problem of knowledge.

HOW ARE OBJECTS KNOWN?

Perhaps the best way to introduce our exploration is first to summarize and then criticize our common sense view of knowledge which has been called "Common Sense Realism." Since it is a view we acquire and hold naturally, some call it "Natural Realism." Since we acquire it naively, or without much critical reflection, it is often called "Naive Realism." Let us adopt this latter name.

Naive Realism

Selecting a table in our room as an object of knowledge, for example, what does common sense tell us about it? It is colored. It has size and shape. It is heavy and it endures. If we leave the room and come back later, it will still be there and will have been there all of the time, unless, of course, someone moves it during our absence. Our looking at it does not affect it, does not change its nature, does not modify it in the least. Its color, size and shape really are just as we see them. We could feel its weight if we lifted it. When many of us look at it, we can all see the same thing.

Generalizing from our natural view of our knowledge of a table to a view about the nature of all objects of knowledge, I quote the following systematic statement of naive realism from *Philosophy, An Introduction.**

> Six statements summarize this doctrine: 1. Objects which are known exist independently of their being known. They can endure or continue to exist without being experienced by anyone. Knowing

---

*Archie J. Bahm, *Philosophy, An Introduction* (Bombay, Asia, 1964), Ch. II. See Part I, Chapters II to XII for an introductory treatment of eleven theories of knowledge.

the objects does not create them. 2. Objects have qualities, or, if one prefers, properties, characteristics or attributes, which are parts of the objects. As qualities of objects, they do not derive their existence or nature from the knower. 3. Objects, including their qualities, are not affected merely by being known. Knowledge of objects in no way changes their nature. 4. Objects seem as they are and are as they seem. Or, as we sometimes say, appearances are realities. What seems obviously so is so. 5. Objects are known directly; that is, there is nothing between them and our knowledge of them. They occur in our experience. We experience them exactly as they are without distortion by any intervening medium. 6. Objects are public; that is, they can be known by more than one person. Several people can see the same object and see it exactly as it is.

Trouble arises for the naive realist when attention is called to the fact that the first and fifth statements are incompatible. Objects are independent of experience and yet they are in experience. Upon reflection, we realize that our experiences, knowledge, ideas, etc., are located somewhere inside our heads. But objects appear to be located outside of our heads. How can objects which are outside one's head be in experience which is inside one's head? How can objects which are known to be some distance away still be known directly when one's knowledge is somewhere within him? How can objects be "out there" and the ideas of objects be "in here" unless they are somehow separated? If separated, how can they be known directly?

Trouble arises for the naive realist also when he faces the fact of error. Errors occur quite commonly. When they are called to our attention, we are happy to recognize them because, by doing so, we then arrive at the truth. But if asked what assurance is there that the new view is true, we reply that it seems true. But this is the same assurance which we had about the error before it seemed to be an error. The naive realist then has no satisfactory account of error, for if things are as they seem and seem as they are, then whatever seems so is so. Error, on such a view, is impossible theoretically, because an error is something which seems so but is not so.

Recall the common experience of seeing a stick partially submerged in water. Upon first sight, the stick appears bent or broken. If naive realism is to be taken at its face value, then if it seems to be bent it is bent. When the stick is pulled from the water, it appears straight. Does the stick bend as it submerges in the water? Our previous experience with sticks and water usually suggests "No." But since the stick appears to bend as it goes in, what can we do to determine whether it is really bent or really straight? For the moment, it seems both bent and straight. Since it cannot be both, one of the two appearances must be erroneous. Note, here, how common sense rejects common sense. That is, it is a matter of common sense that when two contradictory appearances appear, one of them must be rejected. The next step often taken is to slide a hand along the stick down into the water. To the hand the stick seems straight, even though to the eye it seems bent. Most naive realists are satisfied by this experiment. They accept the stick as straight. The bent appearance is dismissed as error or illusion and the matter is dropped. But, we may ask, what are illusions? They consist in being objects which are not as they seem. If objects are not as they seem, then what makes seeming sometimes so and sometimes not so? In what follows, we shall cite many examples to support the contention that the common dismissal of errors as "exceptions to the rule" is itself an error. Error is more common than commonly supposed.

Since psychologists distinguish many kinds of perception in accordance with the types of sensation involved, we may conveniently select representative examples. Although some objects are perceived through the functioning of only one kind of sensory end organ, e.g. through seeing, hearing, tasting or smelling, many others involve more than one. Examples of single-sensory error will be considered first and those of multi-sensory error later.

Error in visual perception is illustrated by railroad tracks which appear to converge at a point in the distance, but which, nevertheless, seem to remain equidistant no matter how far we travel on them. Blood appears blue in veins, red when shed, pale pink or white under a microscope. When plainsmen first venture into high mountains they misjudge distances, traveling miles and miles toward a nearby peak without getting closer. Here, too, mountain streams sometimes seem to flow uphill. Mirages so common on western plains lure the novice to lakes which evaporate upon approach. Mirrors baffle infants just achieving competence in reaching for objects in their world. Rainbows puzzle children who see them "right over there." In movies we see shooting, falling and galloping away, but later the lights reveal only a solid wall or canvas. When western movies were first shown in the West, naive cowboys attending their first movies reacted so realistically, we are told, as to join personally in shooting the villain.

Error in auditory perception is exemplified by first experiences with ringing ears, echoes, striking two keys and hearing only one sound. Gustatory error may be encountered when one eats a large amount of candy. The first piece is sweet and delicious, the fiftieth sour and sickening. Coffee, tobacco and beer which seem bitter at first, become agreeable later. Some foods taste different when we have a cold. Olfactory error can occur, as when the stifling smell, obvious upon entering a closed room, seems to disappear even without its being ventilated after we have remained there a while.

Tactile error perplexes one who, having lost a limb, continues to locate pain or itching in the leg region. We notice pressure of our chair against our skin, whereas only our clothes touch us directly. Kinesthetic errors occur when the same objects appear heavy and light at different times. An empty carton pops up lightly if we had expected it to be full, yet the same carton feels extremely heavy if full when thought to be empty. Errors of equilibrium result from our twirling the body rapidly enough to become dizzy and then stopping suddenly. The world keeps turning in the opposite direction, or the floor comes up with a bang. Thermal error affects us when we have warmed our hands at different degrees of temperature and then plunged them into water of even temperature. To the hot hand the water feels cold and to the cooler hand it feels warm.

Such examples of error trouble the naive realist, but they trouble him very little. He goes from conviction to new conviction, confident in the reliability of each new view. When pressed with the query, "But how can you tell that your new conviction is more reliable than the view given up as erroneous?" he often answers, "Well, I just know." Or, if he is cornered and prodded for an explanation, five kinds of replies eventually come out: he appeals to his other senses for corroboration; he compares his opinion with past experiences; he repeats the experiment; he invokes the testimony of others; he appeals to instruments.

1. If appearances derived through one sensory channel appear contradictory, it is natural to appeal to other senses for corroboration. When one's ears ring unexpectedly, he naturally glances around for the source, but the visual surroundings remain still while the sound seems to move with his head. When one who has lost a leg first experiences an itching as if from his limb, he is impelled to look and to feel whether his leg is still there. The dizzy whirler reaches out toward objects to ascertain whether they whirl as they seem to, and he listens to sounds to determine whether they too revolve. But sometimes different senses contradict each other, though at other times they erroneously corroborate each other. When they contradict, which sense shall we accept as reliable? The half-submerged stick looks bent but feels straight. We hear the distant carpenter's hammer strike once after we see it stop striking. We see lightning flashes now, but hear thunder later. How do we decide between conflicting senses? Are some senses more reliable than others? The naive realist never quite gets around to answering these questions. If we observe him closely, we will find that at some times he relies principally on his eyes and, at other times, on his ears.

When different senses corroborate an error, we are still more baffled. Who has not had the experience of being on a train as it started moving in the railway terminal? First one feels the rumble of wheels over tracks, hears the movement of the wheels under him, and looks out to see that he is, apparently, at last moving. His eyes corroborate his ears and kinesthetic sensations. Then he is startled to find that not his but the next train is moving. In movies we both see and hear gaiety or suffering or excitement, although nothing is really there but light reflected from a canvas. At times we even smell the fragrance of springtime blossoms, shudder at rumbling earthquakes, sway to the swing of music. The marvels of movies remain for the naive realist merely marvels. For, first he is absorbed by the entrancing realities of screen activities and then he devotes himself to the grimmer realities of his own life. But each is real in its turn and while it lasts. So long as he can distinguish one from the other, he does not bother about explaining why. Not only do many of his senses corroborate the reality of movie heroism, but his emotions also lend support through his shedding tears. He is unaware, for the moment, that he has no test of the unreality of the objects of his attention. And he wants none. The same is true in his own life. He is unaware that he has no criterion of the reality or unreality of objects experienced. He has faith in the reality of movie action while it lasts, otherwise he could not really enjoy it. He has faith in his own action, otherwise how could he really enjoy life. But how reliable is such faith?

2. Comparison of present paradoxes with past experiences simply involves greater possibilities of error and greater paradoxes. For past experiences, to be compared, must be remembered. But memory often fails us. What assurance do we have that it is not failing us again? Also, the past experiences themselves may have been erroneous. Can the possibility of erroneous recollection, added to the possibility of erroneous past experience, be used to deny evidence at hand? Perhaps, however, the recollection of experiences repeated many times in the past may be considered more reliable than a single present experience. Yet past experiences may have been erroneous consistently. We may have seen a movie several times and each time the hero married the heroine. Thus, a plurality of past experiences may consistently corroborate a marriage which does not in fact exist. Still greater paradoxes arise when we stop to realize that past experiences themselves no longer exist, and therefore cannot be recalled. Present recollections are present experiences, not past experiences, so what test does one have that his present recollection is like experiences he has had previously? He cannot compare them because past experiences do not exist to be compared with present recollections of them. This fact the naive realist neglects entirely. He thinks he sees directly back into an existing past which in reality has ceased to exist.

3. Doubts sometimes lead to experimentation. Is the bent stick really straight? The naive realist pulls it out, puts it back into the water, and feels it several times to prove that it is really straight. But how can he discount the fact that it also appears bent repeatedly? Also, if past experiences can have been consistently in error, why not present and future experiences? Twirl around again and again and the world will also whirl again and again. The conditions which produce error can themselves be repeated. How can one ever be sure that he is not in error?

4. When doubts become serious, we naturally consult others. Somehow we have come to trust the counsel of others, at least about some things. "Does the stick look bent to you? You feel it and see if it isn't straight." Gregarious naive realists derive much satisfaction from social corroboration, but they fail to realize two things. First, perception of other people as objects to be consulted is itself also liable to error. Most of us have mistaken manikins, mirror images and movie motions for real men. Or, in dreams we have consulted our friends and have gained their agreement. What proof do we have that there are real people to consult? Secondly, even if we actually consult real people, are they not subject to the same errors as we? Cannot people be in agreement and yet be in error? For centuries people agreed that the earth is flat. People having the same kinds of color blindness agree in their discrimination of color. If others share our error, how can we profit by consulting them for proof?

5. The last resort of the naive realist is an appeal to instruments. An immovable half-submerged log is tested by pushing another stick, which is known to be straight, down beside it. Real heat is measured by thermometers. The real size and shape of the table are tested by ruler and square. But this appeal to instruments, like the appeal to other senses, to past experiences, to repetition and to other persons, is a confession of failure. For it is a confession that apparently obvious objects are not self-evident. An appeal to instruments is an appeal to reflection, and to the extent that we are reflective we cease to be naive.

Before we let the naive realist out of his corner, let us ask him one more question: "How can you tell when you are not dreaming?" He replies, "I can pinch myself to see if I am awake." "But can you not dream of pinching yourself and of convincing yourself that you are awake?" "Yes, but I can ask others if I am awake, and I can walk and run and read." "But can you not dream of doing these also?" He is forced to admit this, but he persists in discovering additional suggestions, including that of waking up. But people sometimes dream of waking up and of arousing their friends to settle cooperatively their dreaming doubts. If there is nothing in waking moments about which we cannot dream, and if dreams seem real, then what assurance does one have that he is not now dreaming? The Chinese Taoist philosopher, Chuang Tzu (*c.* 369 to 268 BC), is often quoted as saying: "Once upon a time, I, Chuang Tzu, dreamt I was a butterfly. . . . Suddenly I awaked, and there I lay, myself again. Now I do not know whether I was then a man dreaming I was a butterfly, or whether I am now a butterfly dreaming I am a man."

The foregoing account of naive realism neglected to mention intrinsic values. But the naive realist view is that the table before us seems to have intrinsic value, as suggested, for example, by its rich brown mahogany finish, by its being highly polished, shiny, smooth, with curved carved legs and a top inlaid with coral and gems depicting madonna and child and known to be a rare work of a famous craftsman. The foregoing types of criticisms apply also to his naive view of values. But the point of marshaling so much evidence regarding ordinary perception of shapes and sizes and colors is to make clear that many of the difficulties which people raise about judgments of value are not peculiar to value judgments but are common also to many so-called judgments of fact.

Does it not seem strange, once you stop to think about it, that people who are not at all disturbed about not having a satisfactory theory about knowledge of shapes, sizes and colors of tables become very much disturbed about not having a satisfactory theory about knowledge of values? What, now, is your theory of knowledge? If you can achieve an answer which satisfactorily overcomes all of the doubts properly raised against naive realism, then I suggest that you will find yourself well on your way toward a more satisfactory theory of the knowledge of values. Naive realism is untenable as a theory because it contains self-contradictions which it cannot overcome on its own terms. Hence, one who seeks a tenable theory will have to look farther.

Scientific Realism

We cannot here review the history of epistemologies nor even survey the major types. We select only two for consideration: "Scientific Realism" and "Pragmatism."

"Scientific Realism" is the name sometimes given to that theory

of knowledge which can be constructed from implications of conclusions in several different sciences. In a day when conclusions
in some sciences are taught to beginners with an air of considerable certainty, there is a ready-made tendency for many to give
their assent in advance to such a scientific theory of knowledge.
However, as we shall see, the conclusions of scientists are based
upon assumptions and upon inferences which may themselves be
less certain than the direct intuitions of the naive realist. The
naive realist works with appearances which are directly apprehended. The scientific realist must also depend upon appearances
which are directly apprehended as data serving as evidence for his
theories, but also upon indirect inferences involving many different intricate, highly abstract hypotheses by specialists in widely
differing fields. Criticisms of assurances that our perceptions of
pointer readings on scales or gauges, objects appearing in microscopes or telescopes and computer reports are similar to those
plaguing the naive realist, as we shall see. The scientific realist
too has difficulty proving that he is not dreaming that he is a
scientific realist.

But first, especially for   those who "have faith in science,"
let us attempt a summary reconstruction of scientific realism.

Let us return to our example of a table in our room. Physicists
tell that the light source needed for visual perception consists in
energy activated in such a way that it gives off light waves or
rays which travel through the atmosphere to the surface of the
table where some are absorbed and others reflected. The chemist
explains the chemical composition of pigments in the paint on
the surface and why differences in their nature result in variations
in the way light waves are absorbed and reflected to produce
differences in what we call colors. Light waves reflected from the
surface travel through the air to the skin surface of an eyeball,
some of them penetrating the skin or cornea, passing through a
liquid or aqueous humor, the lens, more liquid or vitreous humor,
and reach the retina or a transparent membrane lining the back
side of the eye and consisting of rods and cones which are cells
serving as electrochemical transformers producing nervous impulses from light waves. Such impulses are transmitted through
ganglion cells, neurones and synapses of the optic nerve to the

cortex of the brain where they excite brain cells already conditioned by previous stimulus-response excitations. There, somehow, such cellular activity produces awareness of an apparent, colored, shaped, three-dimensional table. Despite great success in mapping the geography of the brain and correlations between brain waves and sensory impulses, how and why awareness of objects is produced still remains a complete mystery, so far as I know. Nevertheless, an apparent object emerges in the brain, or in immediate conjunction with it, according to scientific realism.

Now we find scientific realism has two tables to deal with, the one sitting on the floor in our room and the other emerging in awareness in our brain. So the problem of knowledge becomes complicated by how the two tables are known. The one existing in the brain is, of course, intuited or apprehended directly since there is nothing between the apparent table and our knowledge of it, for such knowledge consists in such immediate apprehension. The problem which then faces the scientific realist is how to get the two tables back together again, so to speak, or how to relate and correlate the two different tables and our two different ways of knowing them.

Criticisms of scientific realism are many. The following samples must suffice for our purposes. They can all be stated as related to the problem of truth. For, presumably, we can be sure that we have "true knowledge" of the real table only if we can show that the two tables are essentially alike. But as soon as we begin to try to show likeness, we run into trouble. Start with size: the table top is, let us say, four feet square but our whole brain is less than a foot square and the spot in the cortex where the brain cells are excited may be closer to an inch square. Hence they cannot have the same size, and the problem is obviously more aggravated when we perceive mountains or the moon. They are not made of the same stuff, so to speak, since the table, especially if it is made of metal, consists of chemicals which are quite different in nature from the organic compounds constituting brain cells.

They are unlike in color, and we find involved in at least three different meanings of "color." First, any "color" existing in the real table consists in pigments which are chemicals, or molecules, atoms and subatomic particles of certain kinds; these pigments remain on the table and neither travel to the brain nor exist in the brain in duplication. Secondly, "color" existing as light waves of various definite frequencies depends both upon how these occur in and emanate from the light source, what happens to them as they pass through the air, which ones are reflected by the pigments, what happens to them as the reflected remainder passes through the air and cornea, lens and liquids of the eye. Any "color" existing as light waves ceases when they stimulate the rods and cones, for then transformation from light waves to nerve impulses occurs. Not only will what happens vary with conditions causing color blindness, for there are special cones for each of the primary colors of light which vary in their ability to respond, but since varying rates of restoration of energy in different cells as they become fatigued determine whether and what kind of nervous impulses will be sent on to the brain. Thus, whether the color appearing in our awareness, somewhere in our brain, is in any way like the colorless atoms in pigments, or the colorless light waves which cause awareness of colors, or the colorless nervous impulses, we cannot know but certainly must doubt. Color emerging as an appearance in the brain is created causally by many cooperating sources. That differences in such apparent colors are in some ways correlated with differences in such sources is granted; but what emerges as color in awareness is a unique creation and, except for such correlations, seems to be quite unlike anything in the real table. The problem of both why and how such color appears also as if it were not merely an objective quality of an objective table but a real quality of a real table remains a mystery to the scientific realist.

Ardent scientific realists remain undaunted by these difficulties and turn to the pattern, shape or form of the real table and say that all that is needed for true perception is sameness of form. Critics readily admit that some correlation between the pattern of some elements in the real table and the pattern of impulses reaching the cortex can be demonstrated. But how much, and whether it is enough to admit using the word "true," may be challenged. Even limiting our attention to only the squareness of the table top, we notice first that, unless our eye centered directly above it, the kind of pattern carried through the reflected light waves is not a genuine parallelogram. The light waves themselves vibrate and may be distorted by magnetic or gravitational sources, as is evidenced, for example, in the twinkling of stars. Laws of optics reveal how light waves bend when going from dense to less dense media or vice versa, and what distortions take place as light travels through the cornea, liquids and lens. The pattern of light waves is affected not only by the curvature of the cornea and two sides of the lens but also the curvature of the retina and the different distances through which rays must travel in lens and liquids, and by the fact that some of them reach the blind spot where neither rods nor cones exist and many terminate between the rods and cones which are themselves distributed unevenly both in relative quantity and in density. How the bits of pattern which remain can be transformed without distortion through the electro-chemical processes in the rods and cones, each of which responds in terms of its own constituents and their replenishment, into many separate nervous impulses traveling through successions of neurones connected by synapses with variable resistances and still arrive undistorted is hard to believe. Furthermore, rays passing through the pupil and lens reverse themselves so that the pattern at the retina is upside down relative to the original table. Binocular vision involves two retinal patterns, not just one, and these two must somehow remerge after the two separate bundles of neurones wind and bend through the two optic nerves which join and then each split in half so that half the neurones from one eye and half from the other eye go to the cortex located in one of the two occipital lobes which are separated by a deep fissure. How is it possible for patterns divided in half by this process to reappear whole when the two lobes in which the portions terminate are so divided spatially? The lines of the form of the table appearing in awareness are continuous and unbroken, even though we can trace many discontinuities through different light waves, different rods, different neurones. It becomes evident that what appears in awareness is a mental construct or creation which, though caused in part by conditions in the supposedly real table, is very little like it, even with respect to continuity of line, for the real table is supposed to be composed of atoms which not only differ from each other discontinuously but also consist more of space than nuclei and other particles. Despite admission of some correlation, the scientific realist's explanation of how the two tables are alike even in form encounters so many difficulties as to leave us with more mysteries than answers.

Furthermore, it fails to explain why the table appearing inside the head appears as if it were the other table outside the head. If there are two, why does there appear to be only one? Why do we locate the apparent table as if it were there outside our head? Evidently the apparent table, including its apparent size, color and shape, is a mental construct which appears both as an object of attention and as if it were a real thing. That is, even the primary qualities of size and shape, as well as the secondary qualities of color, are objectified and reified in ordinary perception. It should not be surprising, then, that other qualities, such as tableness representing conceptual contributions, and goodness or beauty representing contributions by our feelings and emotions, are also attributed to the apparent table and projected as if existing out there as real qualities of the real table. Intrinsic value occurring as pleasant feeling, for example, is not shape or size or color, but its appearing as if located in a real table (so that we say that "That's a pleasing table") is no more mysterious, surely, than the way shapes, sizes and colors appear so located. Mystery as to why and how apparent objects occur, and occur appearing as if real, in the first place is admitted. But this mystery is rooted in the nature of man and is not something which can be eliminated by scientific realism. However, the evidence assembled, even in this very sketchy outline, should be enough to demonstrate that differences in the way in which intrinsic values appear as if in real objects and the ways in which so-called factual characteristics, such as sizes, shapes and colors, appear as if in real objects are not so greatly different as critics of axiology, aesthetics and ethics as sciences claim.

Let us explore how feelings may come to be attributed to apparently real objects. Although the accounts of scientific realism with which I am acquainted usually omit such explorations, I see little more difficulty in dealing with feelings than with colors, once an adequate theory about the physiological nature and conditions of feeling has been adopted. One theory, which no doubt has undergone considerable refinement since it orginated several decades ago, is that feelings of enjoyment, sometimes called "positive feeling tone," occur while synaptic resistance between neurones is being reduced and that feelings of discomfort occur when such synaptic resistances are being increased. Many of the causes and conditions of such increase and decrease are already known. Once we overlook the common mystery of how such physiological conditions cause feelings of enjoyment and suffering to emerge into awareness, then the question of why we locate the intrinsic values which they constitute as if in real things is no more mysterious than why we locate apparent size, shape and color in them.

Even if scientific realism neglects the issue, many aestheticians have developed a convenient, and already familiar, language for dealing with the problem. The English word "empathy" and the German word *einfuhlung,* literally meaning "in-feeling" or "feeling into," were coined to describe how beauty and other forms of value occurring within our awareness located inside our heads are projected by us in our acts of thinking and perceiving into objects which then also appear as if real. The vast literature pertaining to *einfuhlung* appears to have been largely neglected by scientific realists.

Pragmatism

Turning from scientific realism which, despite its wide appeal in an age when people idealize science, is not so popular with scientists, we turn next to pragmatism. Pragmatism too is a philosophy of science and of scientific method. It was forged by professional philsophers attempting to deal with difficulties, not only in naive and scientific realisms and a whole history of previous and competing theories of knowledge and science, but also with difficulties in politics, education, psychology, physics, logic, mathematics, etc., which are due to unresolved problems of knowledge.

Pragmatism is basically a theory about how to go about solving problems. It is primarily a theory about method, rather than a set of conclusions about the nature of man and the world. It does not begin by assuming that in an act of knowing, there is a "real" world out there. But, then, neither does it begin by assuming that there is no "real" world out there or that it cannot be known. Methodologically, the pragmatic method begins by being open-minded about what shall be found. But it does begin by assuming that each person is a biological being faced with problems, not the least of which is survival. Although metaphysical, including physical and biological, presuppositions underlying such a methodolgy can be pointed out, pragmatists regard these presuppositions as justifiable in terms of pragmatic methods.

How are objects known according to pragmatism? First of all, we begin as naive realists, accepting appearances as they appear. If the table in our room appears as if real, solid, square, colored and good, we accept such appearances at their face value, so to speak, until some problem arises. Problems of error, whether originating in perception, conception or communication (as in disputes about value, color or solidity), challenge appearances. Doubts about appearances arise and persist. But since we do not enjoy doubting, we attempt to settle our doubts.* We look for suggestions which will explain the apparent discrepancies among appearances. We experiment with alternative hypotheses. We may or may not find a satisfactory solution, and so long as we do not, we keep our mind open and hold our beliefs tentatively. It is this willingness to remain open-minded and tentative which characterizes pragmatism as a method, and which provides a clue to its proposals regarding workable theories in physics, mathematics, values and ethics.

No better introduction to pragmatism as a method exists than in John Dewey's book, *How We Think*.† His "analysis of a complete act of thought" yields five distinguishable steps: (i) a felt difficulty; (ii) its location and definition; (iii) suggestions of possible solution; (iv) development by reasoning of the bearings of the suggestion; (v) further observation and experiment leading to its acceptance or rejection; that is, the conclusion of belief or disbelief.‡ Note that these same five steps, some of which may be

---

*See Charles Sanders Peirce, essays on "How to Make Our Ideas Clear" and "The Fixation of Belief."
†John Dewey, *How We Think* (Boston, Heath, 1910).
‡*Ibid.*, p. 72.

repeated several times, may be distinguished in dealing with both the simplest personal problem ("Did I put a handkerchief in my pants pocket this morning? I thought I did but I see no bulge as usual.") and the most complex physical problem ("The accepted principle of symmetry seems to call for the existence of anti-matter."), and with values ("Would I enjoy the tennis or swimming course more this semester?") and ethics ("Ought I buy a new or used car for my first one?"). The more one becomes acquainted with the work of practicing scientists, the more he realizes how thoroughly they are immersed in dealing with "working hypotheses," i.e. guesses as to how problems are to be solved, and with theories held with a tentative attitude. The scientific attitude, which is essential to the scientific method, requires one to remain open-minded regarding all of his conclusions, partly because we have learned from bitter past experiences that new doubts are likely to arise regarding those conclusions which we once regarded as most certain. People who demand dogmatic answers from scientists, whether physicists or ethicists, do not understand the nature of science.

How are objects known? Once doubts arise, our beliefs about objects become tentative hypothese about the nature. Ideas which "worked" while we were naive realists no longer work, or at least not so well. The various complicated theories called upon by the scientific realist also work to a certain extent for those who are acquainted with them; but they also do not work with complete satisfaction so long as we remain alert to their difficulties. By shifting expectations from solutions which are final, fixed, unchanging and both eternally and universally true, which result from wishful thinking as well as from claims made by earier physicists and ethicists, to solutions which are relative to the problems while they last and accepted tentatively relative to the evidence for and against them thus far available, we come to regard our beliefs about objects as constantly on trial. True ideas are those which work. But each working idea, including your ideas that the table is solid, square, useful or beautiful, "appears less a solution than as a program for more work, and more particularly as an indication of the ways in which existing realities may be changed."*

"The true is only the expedient in the way of our thinking, just as the right is only the expedient in the way of our behaving."†
"Expedient" means fits the needs of the situation whether momentary or in the long run, "for what meets expediently all the experience in sight won't necessarily meet all farther experiences equally satisfactorily."‡ "To continue thinking unchallenged is, ninety-nine times out of a hundred, our practical substitute for knowing in the completed sense."§ Hence, for pragmatism, the way objects are known is always on trial. This holds true for our beliefs about tables, about electrons, about dollars, about the intrinsic value of feelings of satisfaction, about ideals and about feelings of obligation.

The table in front of me appears smooth when I look at it. My physicist friend says the smoothness is illusory. So I put my fingers on it and move them about, receiving tactile sensations which I interpret as smooth. But he objects and gets out a microscope and says "Look." I look and find that it appears to be very rough. Doubts about my unaided eye and fingers arise. He then explains the atomic theory about the regulated movement of particles in solids such that the relative regularity of the action of such particles at the surface of the table produces sensations of smoothness despite their dynamic motions and the comparatively vast areas of space between them. Since I have learned to trust the views of my physicist friend because of successes he has had in solving other problems for me, such trust now bolsters my doubts about my experience of smoothness. The table top is not really smooth. It only seems so. However, when I look at it again and touch it again, it still does seem so.

Those who regard the principle of excluded middle as a "necessary law of nature" rather than as a working hypothesis will say that it cannot be both smooth and not smooth at the same time. You have to give up one or the other view. Some then accept the

---

*William James, *Pragmatism* (New York, Longmans, Green, and Co., 1907), p. 53.
†William James, *The Meaning of Truth* (New York, Longmans, Green, and Co., 1910), p vii.
‡*Ibid.*
§*Ibid.*, p. 116.

atomic theory and claim that ordinary perceptions are false; some choose to retain their common sense views and regard the seemingly absurd claims by scientists as a huge hoax. The pragmatist, on the other hand, when faced with these two conflicting knowledge claims, points out that the seemingly conflicting conclusions are not contradictory but they are solutions to two different kinds of problems, which, momentarily during our discussion, we confused. If by "smoothness" you mean the way a surface feels when touched, then, when I say that the table top is smooth, what I mean is that if and when I touch it I will receive the smooth sensation that I expected, then since I did receive that smooth sensation, my belief or knowledge claim was true. But if by "smoothness" you mean absence of comparatively huge gaps of space between dynamic particles, then the surface is not smooth, and my physicist's belief and knowledge claim may well also be true.

Truth, then, is always relative to beliefs which arise as responses to particular problems, and what makes the belief true or false depends in part upon peculiarities inherent in the circumstances under which the belief emerges and is held. My own refinement upon various versions of pragmatic theories of truth is:

> Each judgment is made with such specifications as are required by its peculiar set of conditions. And such possible specifications as are unintended are irrelevant. The judger alone knows what he is judging and what it would take to make his judgment true. The specifications involved in a judgment may be simple or complex, definite or ambiguous, vague or clear. . . . The truth of each judgment depends upon whether there are whatever specifications are judged to be.*

Returning to the question opening this chapter, namely, "How are values known?" let us examine more remarks about our table. "That's a good table," I say to my friend. He objects: "Values are not real qualities of real tables. All values are subjective or in your mind. To attribute goodness to a real table is to make a false statement." "But," I say, "you yourself judged it to be good because you laid your books on it rather than on that rickety one over there." "Well, you can say it is useful; but that's only because

---

*The generic theory of truth. *The Personalist*, 28:373, Autumn 1947.

I had a use for it. There is no property in the table itself, whether viewed as a solid, extended, colored shape or as a conglomeration of atoms, which can be called 'usefulness.' Without a user there is no usefulness." "Granted this," I reply, "but there is no solidity or color without a toucher or viewer either, according to your atomic theory, and there is no assurance that there are atoms in it either apart from persons holding such a theory and believing that certain kinds of subjectively apprehended evidence derived from beliefs about solid and extended guages, etc. It is because you find the atomic theory useful that you attribute an atomic nature to this table. There is no atomic theory apart from atomic theorists. You make your judgment that the table is made of atoms because you find this to be a more useful theory for certain purposes."

Thus far, our examination is designed to call attention to how instrumental values are attributed to real things and to how the truth and falsity of such judgments of attribution are also relative to the purposes of the attributer. The truth of the belief that "That table is good for holding books" can be tested by trying to put books on it. The truth of the belief that nothing resembling goodness or utility can be found by looking among the atomic particles will depend, I presume, upon someone looking and not finding, or, more indirectly, upon such a belief failing to find support when someone inquires whether it might be conherent with other aspects of the atomic theory. Even if the latter could be shown to be true in the context of atomic theory, it would have no relevance to the more easily provable truth of the claim that the table is indeed of such a nature that if you put books on it it will hold the books. If this is what a judger means by saying "That's a good table," then his judgment can be proved true or false.

Turning from instrumental to intrinsic values, I continue: "That table is beautiful." (Let us assume that "beauty" will serve as an example of intrinsic value for present purposes.) When my friend objects again, "Analyze the table physically or chemically as much as you wish, you will never find beauty or intrinsic value anywhere among its constituents," I interrupt impatiently. "But I like its highly polished, shiny, smooth, rich brown mahogany finish. It's beautiful to me, no matter what your analysis may reveal. Surely you must think it more beautiful than that scratched, warped, broken table out in the alley." He complains, "The light reflection hurts my eyes. That brown color is too dark and looks dirty to me. I'm afraid to use it because my tools might dent it and I would have to pay damages." Our disagreement is of two sorts which, in the heat of argument, may not be clearly distinguished. First, our judgments of attribution differ because our purposes differ when I refer to the way the table appears to me and he refers to an atomic theory about its composition. Both judgments may be true relative to our different purposes because our interests and capacities differ. If we take time to sympathize with each other's purposes, we might say, "If you liked mahogany as much as I do, then you would see it as beautiful too; and when I am carrying tools, I avoid it too."

Objects are known, then, not merely as entities existing independently of knowers, as we often regard them, but also as objects for subjects whose nature depends as much upon the subject who objectifies his ideas, purposes and feelings in his process and act of perception. Awareness of subjective conditions and aspects of knowing objects leads some to conclude hastily that, therefore, objects are purely subjective. Some empiricists (Hume), idealists (Berkeley) and phenomenalists (Kant) abandon attempts to deal with real things as objects of knowledge. But pragmatists willingly take account of both subjective and real conditions of knowing objects, and the distinctions between subjective, objective and real conditions of knowing themselves serve as important ingredients in hypotheses about the nature of knowing and the nature of science. Pragmatism as a philosophy of science begins by assuming that all, or all practical, knowledge arises because people have problems and problems are obviously subjective. To fail to keep the subjective conditions constantly in mind is to fail to have an adequate theory of objects, regardless of whether the size, shape, color, utility, beauty, a complex gestalt of these or none of these is at stake. When one holds a philosophy of science which neglects or, worse, denies the essential role of subjective factors in the formation of objects, he has difficulty dealing with values as objects. But pragmatism as a philosophy of science has no such difficulty. Values, including intrinsic values, behave in experience in much the same way as other aspects of objects.

(Acceptance of both subjective and real factors as essentially interinvolved in the production of objects is seemingly more complicated than explaining objects entirely in terms of either subjective or real factors alone. But if, or since, both and their interdependent interaction are needed for an adequate explanation, acceptance of both is really the simplest adequate theory. Just as physicists have sought to eliminate either the wave or the particle theory of light but have learned that, no matter how uncomfortable they are with the greater complexity, acceptance of a theory recognizing both wave and particle kinds of behavior as essential to the nature of light is necessary for an adequate view. Why some people demand simple explanations in value theory when they are willing to accept more complex theories elsewhere when needed remains a bit of a mystery.)

DO VALUES BEHAVE?

The term "behaviorism" has been used to name several different kinds of theories. When popularized by psychologist John B. Watson, it denoted a materialistic theory of behavior. According to this theory, the universe consists entirely of matter (i.e. "matter and energy") so man, as a part of the universe, also consists entirely of matter (as against "mind" which was advocated by idealists and dualists). So, in the absence of any mind (or soul or psyche), psychology had to concern itself entirely with how man, the machine — albeit a living, stimulus-response machine — behaved. Psychology, originally the science of the soul, became the science of human behavior, or, since animals also behave as stimulus-response mechanisms much as man does, the science of behavior.

But many pragmatists also adopted the term "behavior," and in doing so first broadened its use to name the way anything behaves in experience. Pragmatism, as a theory of method, accepted whatever suggested itself as relevant to the solution of any problem which arose as functioning or behaving as a factor in the solution of, or in the failure to solve, that problem. In this broadened usage, obviously apparent values behave. And both subjective, objective and apparently real factors function behaviorally, as do their interactions, for their ways of interacting may also be observed to persist, vary and perhaps even cease in ways which must be recognized in any fully adequate theory of behavior. In this sense, values do behave. So no behavioral science is adequate which overlooks not only the behavior of values but also the multiplicities of ways in which they behave.

For example, my preference for rich brown mahogany furniture is a persisting trait of my character and, under conditions where I find appropriate opportunity for pausing to appreciate a piece of furniture as appealing to my preference, I am likely to say, "My, that's beautiful!" That is, my own tendency to enjoy experiencing the appearance of a rich brown mahogany as an apparent quality of an apparently real table is an observable character trait which persists, or behaves in a persistent manner, relative to the occurrence of such opportunities. One could study the relative persistence of my preference and note how consistently it remains and varies in the presence of alternative colors, even as furniture marketing experts do relative to the large sections of population in which they sell their products more or less successfully. Thus subjective factors, including enjoyments, function behaviorally in experience in scientifically observable ways. That I tend to objectify my enjoyment by attributing the beauty I experience to the apparently real object when I am not focusing attention upon its subjectivity is also something observable. The naturalness and normalcy of such objectification in all people, even after they have become aware of criticisms of naive realism, is a scientifically observable phenomenon. And the roles of apparently real causal factors in producing experiences of beauty, e.g. of mahogany furniture, are already well known as evidenced by the speeds of changing frames acceptable in movie projectors. The behavior if intrinsic values as factors in experience is already well known and exploited by those interested in movie box office receipts. Why there is a reluctance on the part of some so-called scientists to recognize such readily observable behavior is something of a mystery, unless we attribute it to ignorance or to prejudicial habits which are also scientifically observable phenomena.

Axiology as a pure science is concerned with universal generalization about values, not with particulars as such except as illustrations. Pragmatism is a method for dealing with both particular problems and problems in pure science when, and because, they also become problems for particular people. As a pure science, axiology investigates the nature of values, i.e. the ways in which values behave, both ways in which all value situations are alike and ways in which all value situations of the major particular kinds are alike.

In sum, ways in which all value experiences are alike include the following: (1) All are alike in being value experiences. (2) All are alike in involving both intrinsic and instrumental values, directly or indirectly. (3) If our analysis is correct, all intrinsic values are alike (a) in being present in awareness, when existing, (b) in being intuited or apprehended directly, (c) in being felt, i.e. enjoyed or suffered, in some degree, (d) in being either one or more of our four kinds, either in pure or blended forms (e.g. one may enjoy the color of mahogany the first time one sees it, exemplifying pleasing sensation; youth anticipating marriage and home may enjoy enthusiasm at the prospect of owning mahogany furniture; the homeowner may enjoy a feeling of satisfaction with his paid-for mahogany furniture; and the aged may feel that retaining possession of his long-loved mahogany contributes to his contentment). (4) All are alike in being objectified, or in behaving as objects, or aspects of objects, of attention (with possible yogic exceptions). Awareness of a distinction between apparent and real objects is not essential to value experiences; however, attention to the distinction is of major, even crucial, importance in practical situations involving comparative judgments, decisions and, as we shall see later, feelings of obligation.

CHAPTER 5

POTENTIAL VALUES

IN WHAT WAYS ARE VALUES POTENTIAL?

A LL ACTUAL INTRINSIC VALUES, i.e. feelings of enjoying or suffering, exist now, not at some other time, past or future. But what is present passes quickly, and whether we shall be enjoying or suffering much or little at the next moment and in the foreseeable future interests most of us most of the time. If we believe ourselves to be helpless, we may feel able to do little more than hope for the best. But most of us most of the time believe that causes have consequences and that how we act may have a bearing upon whether our future experiences are more or less enjoyable. We have learned from past experience that when faced with certain kinds of situations we are more likely to experience enjoyment or avoid suffering if we act in one way rather than in another. When removing hot coals from a fire, it is better to take hold of them with a tongs than with bare fingers.

All of our concerns for future feelings presuppose that there will be such feelings which are not now actual. One might suggest, facetiously to be sure, that if future values are not actual values they do not now exist, so why should we concern ourselves with what does not exist? But regardless of what we discover about the biological provisions for our interest in survival, growth and reproduction, we surely have also learned from personal experience that we do have desires and that desires are by nature for something which we do not now have and which we can expect to have fulfilled only in the future (even the desire to continue enjoying present values involves continuing into the future). To experience desire is to be concerned for future fulfillment. Even the enjoying of enthusiasm or desirousness as an intrinsic value cannot exist apart from the future-orientedness of the desire. And the end-in-itself character of our present enjoyment, although it needs nothing more to be experienced as enjoyment, often induces in us a desire for more of it, and when it does, it also serves as an additional instrumental value.

To the extent that we are concerned about future values, i.e. intrinsic values which are not now actual, we are concerned with values which are called "potential," though this is a tricky word as we shall see. Since, apparently, intrinsic values cannot exist unless caused to exist, and since all causes of intrinsic values are means or instruments and are therefore called "instrumental values," our concern for future values involves us in concern for instrumental values insofar as we are aware of having some control over them. But, although present actual instruments which will cause future intrinsic values are the powers, or have in them the potency or potentiality to bring such future intrinsic values into existence, they are not in themselves potential intrinsic values. Immediately we can see that the word "potential" as customarily used, is misapplied to future intrinsic values because they do not already exist as intrinsic values in the causes which bring them about. Our customary usage derives from Aristotelian conceptions of natures as static, such that the essence of the oak tree is already fully present in the acorn; but now that we believe natures to be much more dynamic and their development to be a result of multi-plicities of essential causes, all of which together are the power or potentiality needed to bring about future actualization, it is improper, strictly speaking, to refer to future intrinsic values as now potential. Yet we do have a need for speaking about such future intrinsic values now, so until a more suitable vocabulary gains common currency we shall doubtless continue to speak as if future intrinsic values were now potential.

Notice that we have practical needs for objectifying our ideas of future intrinsic values, for otherwise we would not be aiming at them and putting forth efforts to achieve them if we could not regard them as objects to aim at. And, as naive realists, we tend to treat apparently future intrinsic values as if they now had some sort of future reality. That is, we behave as if their supposed future actuality were now already a "potential" reality. And so long as we operate as naive realists, we can speak as if such "potential" intrinsic values behave as goals for our endeavors. The ways in which goals function in directing endeavors are observable phenomena which can be, and have been, studied by scientific methods. Since most of our ideas about values are intricately bound up with other features of our experience, goals projected occur usually as gestalts in which the intrinsic value aspects are not always clearly distinguished. Hence, many of our studies of goals, preferences and ideals are stated in terms of incompletely analyzed gestalts and in ways in which the strictly intrinsic value aspects remain unclear. But, even so, the behavioral role of ideas of goals is well known. More careful distinguishing of intrinsic value aspects of such ideas may result in more precise measurements in statistical studies of goal-directed behavior and, so to speak, of the behavior of goals in directing endeavors.

WHY ARE POTENTIAL VALUES IMPORTANT?

Without pursuing further in this introductory summary of ethics as a behavioral science the complicated issues at stake in understanding actuality and potentiality, let us survey some reasons why such understanding is important for ethics and other value sciences depending upon it.

Ethics

First of all, when a person faces actual decisions—such as shall I marry Jean or Jane, become a banker or teacher, buy antique mahogany or modern plastic—he is involved in evaluating ends, means and probabilities that the means will bring about the ends. Future ends, although they will occur as moments of enjoyment, are pictured as gestalts, not merely of an evening's birthday party or a day of intimate family living, but as a flow of weeks, months and years of variable happiness. Such alternative complexes of ideas about future intrinsic values are now only envisioned "potentialities" which, when the time comes for their actualization, may be quite different from the ways anticipated. So when one chooses between apparently better or worse ends, he is choosing among presently apparent potentialities. But after an end has been chosen, one still has to make judgments about which are the better or worse means to that end. These means, too, are present apparent potentialities, but if the things chosen fail to bring about the end, then they were not in fact means to that end. So, one also has to judge whether or not things, even presently actual things, will in fact become means, i.e. whether or not they have the potential instrumental value. It is no wonder that people feel forced to rely on hunches, impulses or the advice of others in making complicated decisions when they do not normally clearly distinguish between means and ends, let alone between the merely probably potential means and ends and the not yet existing means and ends, while naively objectifying all of them as having reality. Yet mistakes in any one of these areas may crucially prevent realization.

Secondly, knowledge of probabilities which can be gained by personal experience tends to help in providing sounder judgments. Hence, one discovers the value of training, developing skills, reliable habits, character traits, all of which may come under the general heading of "education," in providing resources for making better decisions. All such habits or skills may actually serve as means whenever they are called into use in achieving ends.

Thirdly, customs, mores, institutions and laws are intended to serve as means for maintaining group welfare. Acceptable standards of social behavior, whether fads or enforced, are not intrinsic values, but are instruments for guiding judgment and action. To the extent that they do influence opinion and behavior, they do have actual power; and to the extent that they stand ready to do so when needed, they may be said to have conditional potentiality or to behave as conditional potential instrumental values. They function as bases for conditional oughts.

Fourthly, ethics, even as a pure science, extends beyond generalizations about factors which are alike in all ethical situations, and has as part of its task exploration of the multitudes of kinds of conditional potential instrumental values. That all other sciences are concerned with the nature of things, i.e. how things behave, does not excuse ethicists as scientists from attending to the need for showing how all such ways in which things behave may also function as conditional potential instrumental values. In whatever way any cause or condition, or any uniformity regarding any kind of cause or condition, may enter into the consideration of any person when making an actual choice, it functions as a conditional potential instrumental value. Principles for choosing include principles for choosing among instrumental values, and as life in megalopolis becomes more complicated, more and more of our choices seem to be devoted to such choices.

Economics

The "goods and services" with which economics deals are conditional potential instrumental values which have their bases in desires for potential intrinsic values and which, for convenience, economists call "wants." Whether they be "hardware," "software" or "dry goods," things useful in satisfying wants attain "economic value" by virtue of "scarcity" (where "demand" exceeds "supply") and "exchangeability." Thus economic value is a much more restricted kind of value than instrumental value, but economic values are also values attributed to things which serve as instruments, actually or potentially. "Exchange value" is the value attributed to anything when it is offered in exchange for some other goods or services, directly or indirectly. That is, if I am willing to trade you two bushels of pears for one bushel of plums during the harvest season, the exchange value of a bushel of apples in terms of plums is two bushels on that occasion. Exchange value is often spoken of in terms of "price." Price may be determined by bargaining or may be established as a "fixed price."

Once some kind of instrument can serve as a relatively stable unit and is exchangeable for many different kinds of things, we call this "money." Money in the form of coins, e.g. gold coins, was held to have value because the metal could be melted and used for gold ornaments. Then paper money, or promissory notes guaranteed by some government, was introduced as an additional kind of instrument, but its value depended, and depends, upon the ability and reliability of the government. Unfortunately for general value theory, the term "intrinsic value" was attributed to gold coins because the metal had other economic uses whereas the value of the paper serving as paper money has almost no such value. Confusion of the two different meanings of "intrinsic value," i.e. the additional potential instrumental value which gold metal has and feelings of enjoyment, can lead only to misunderstanding. The fact that many people, especially misers, do experience enjoyment when viewing coins or bars and objectify their feelings as if in the coins as real things, thereby experiencing actual intrinsic value at the same time they are looking at real coins, brings the two kinds of intrinsic value in close conjunction, at least, and uncritical judgment is likely to identify them. When coins are also decorated with artistic designs, the enjoyment one has in viewing the design may also be fused with his other enjoyments. Without help from axiological technicians in pointing out and clarifying the numerous distinctions and kinds of value involved, people remain confused and this continuing confusion serves as part of the confusion people have about values and ethics.

Economic values are complicated further, not merely by fluctuations in value of money when exchanged for foreign currencies, but especially by the development of credit systems for delayed payment of debts for exchanged goods, banks, banking systems, loans, interest and service charges, to say nothing of taxes and insurance costs, and now the flourishing "credit card" system and computerized accounting and billing. Each additional step in such a process adds a new kind of conditional potential instrumental value which needs to be taken into account when calculating costs. As these steps and conditioning factors multiply, the distance of the kind of monetary value experienced as objectified in observing a numerical symbol in a monthly bank balance, for example, from the hard or soft goods which serve as instruments which may or may not result in actually enjoyed intrinsic value tends to increase. These complexifications do not change the fact that the whole monetary and economic system has its value basis ultimately in the feelings of enjoyment or suffering of particular individuals at particular times. But correlations become more difficult to observe as that distance increases. Hence the need for greater emphasis in educational systems on learning to understand the nature of values, including economic values, should be obvious if we expect people to be more intelligently self-directing.

The importance for ethical theory and practice of understanding economic theory and practice may be noted relative to decisions, not merely of individuals but of organized groups, such as governments and corporations, regarding the production, distribution and consumption of goods (things having potential instrumental value). "Waste" is a general term for numerous kinds of economic evils pertaining to such goods or "wealth." Waste may occur in almost every phase of the production, distribution, consumption process. We may overproduce or underproduce, overdistribute or underdistribute, overconsume or underconsume.

Overproduction results in things which could serve as instruments (conditioned potential values) if they were used, but as soon as they cannot in fact so serve, even their conditional potentiality is gone. For example, spare parts for cars may be manufactured but never distributed, distributed but not sold, sold but not put in a car, or put in a car which is never driven. The enjoyment aimed at, albeit indirectly, in making such parts is aborted; and all efforts (and any suffering felt) connected with such making, etc., are wasted. Underproduction may cause even greater waste, as when whole automobiles must be junked because no spare parts are available.

Overdistribution, giving people more of certain instruments than they can use, and underdistribution, failing to make existing instruments available to persons who need them desperately in order to utilize other available resources essential to life, also causes waste.

Overconsumption of goods—such as buying more clothes than one can wear or more perishable food then one can eat, or eating foods in quantities which produce overweight, lethargy or other disabilities—and underconsumption of goods—such as saving for future enjoyment goods which are needed for present health maintenance without which no future enjoyment can be—are causes of waste. Such obvious examples of personal waste typify a kind of problem which attains horrendous dimensions when viewed in terms of populations of nations or the world.

The role of managers as instrumental values, and of the wisdom of their decisions in predicting needs and facilitating the production and flow of goods, becomes more apparent as economic processes become more intricate and more world-wide. Their roles, and hence conditional potential values, change somewhat as we shift from an economy of scarcity to an economy of abundance, or, as we exhaust irreplaceable natural resources, from an economy of abundance to an economy of scarcity. Awareness that human intelligence has developed to the place where now it is possible to invent not only substitutes but whole new kinds of resources puts a premium upon utilization of inventive abilities. Some say we have now entered a new age, the Age of Creativity, where the conditional potentiality of persons for creating new ways of creating additional kinds and quantities of instruments with conditional potential value is itself a most basic kind of conditional potential value; all may profit from the results of such exploitation as well as those who, when so exploited, enjoy enhanced feelings of enthusiasm, satisfaction and contentment during and after behaving as creators. As the management of men—by assuring them opportunities for exercising their creative capacities—becomes a more central concern of economics (and of government, business and education), the roles of axiology and ethics as behavioral sciences in extending our understanding of the many kinds of both actual and potential intrinsic and instrumental values, and the obligations which emerge from such understanding, come to be regarded as much more important.

Too often both consumer and producer forget what many economists and business managers know, namely that despite the distances and often weak correlations between the values at different levels in the intrinsic value, instrumental value, exchange value, price, etc., hierarchy, the processes involved often behave like traffic on a two-way street.

1. Businessmen interested in increasing profits by increasing the number of sales of consumer goods have discovered that satisfied customers repeat their purchases more often than dissatisfied customers; hence they seek to promote customer satisfaction (enjoyment of intrinsic value) for this purpose, thereby using such satisfaction as a means to increasing sales, profits and their own satisfactions. Their satisfaction with such increased profits in turn

motivates them to provide still further customer satisfaction in seeking more satisfaction for themselves. When people use methods of increasing each other's intrinsic values as means to increasing their own intrinsic values, the economy and the society may be said to be "healthy," or, aphoristically, "healthy, wealthy and wise."

2. Persons trusting their experiences with relatively close correlations between satisfactions resulting from purchases of goods from reliable companies and competition-determined price tags tend to accept the price as a moderately reliable index to anticipated intrinsic value. When this is the case, artificial raises in price may then cause customers, naively objectifying their ideas and feelings of instrumental and intrinsic value in the objects as perceived, to impute greater value to them. If the resulting feelings of satisfaction are greater, then both salesman and customer may feel such greater satisfaction warrants the artificial raise in price, as is often the case where merchants specialize in "catering to class."

3. The introduction and mass distribution of credit cards and computerized credit accounting connected with automated payroll deduction services represents a great adventure in facilitating spending and borrowing which challenges the ingenuity of agents responsible for maintaining safety in our managed economy. When significant variation in the ways in which factors, old or new, causally influence all other value factors and threaten viability, manifest on a large scale as "inflation" or "depression," counter measures become needed. Current gyrations in stock prices, interest rates and wages make all of us more conscious of the instrumental values of both novel techniques and of economy management methods. Increase in ethical responsibilities of policy makers who, whether fortunately or unfortunately, exist and function now at many different levels and in many different areas of our economy, is something of which we become increasingly aware. Since this is so, increasing understanding of the intricate natures of both economic processes, intrinsic and instrumental value processes, and ethical processes is needed by all. To regard economic processes as somehow mechanically self-adjusting, and to fail to keep conscious of the essentially human bases of all potential values is to invite disaster.

4. The role of philosophy as a potential instrumental value tends to be overlooked. Its significance often receives attention in periods of extreme poverty and extreme wealth. I single out one aspect of philosophy, namely the wisdom of knowing when one has had enough. Wanting more than one can get, whether because poor or because rich (the rich surfeited with potential instrumental values which cannot all be enjoyed because of the limited capacity of the human body to sustain enjoyment), is always a cause of suffering. The potential instrumental value of desire as a cause of evil is too often neglected. A scientifically sound principle for the management of desire was worked out during the sixth century BC by Gotama, the Buddha: "Desire for what will not be attained ends in frustration; therefore to avoid frustration, avoid desiring what will not be attained."*

The economic value of techniques for facilitating contentment, for which many religious institutions are designed, is another area for ethical concern about potential values. The sluggish degeneration of medieval dogmatic explanations during a period of widespread zip-speed institutional changes, together with the lack of new commitment-commanding ideals needed for megalopolitan morale, is causing moral chaos and a moral vacuum. Failure to develop ethics as a behavioral science by those committed to scientific understanding and management of our economy is itself potential instrumental value (i.e. evil), which, hopefully, publication of this volume may help to relieve.

Politics

Ownership of goods is itself a good, or evil; systems of social control, favoring private or public ownership and equal or unequal distribution of ownership, together with the rights and duties relative thereto are good or evil potential instrumental values. Establishment of political institutions enabling more people to enjoy more "freedoms" thereby behaviorally activates potential instrumental values. Since keeping such institutions efficient has a rather direct bearing upon the availability of such values, pursuits of policies enabling intelligent revision as well as sensitive enforcement

---

*See Archie J. Bahm, *Philosophy of the Buddha.* Harper, 1958, p. 15.

of provisions for guaranteeing such rights, privileges, opportunities and their correlative duties, also functions as potential value. The importance of political science to ethics and of ethics as a science to politics needs stressing. The achievements in each science provide conditional potential values useful to the other.

WHY ARE THE POTENTIAL VALUES OF LIFE IMPORTANT?

The reason why values, both intrinsic and instrumental, are important is that they are important for life. The value of a life may be examined, i.e. both its intrinsic value and its instrumental value.

Intrinsic Value of Life

If intrinsic goodness consists in feelings of enjoyment, then axiomatically the greater the enjoyment experienced by a person the greater the intrinsic goodness of his life. Such a view involves holding that the greater the suffering experienced by a person the greater the intrinsic evil of his life. Since all people have feelings of both enjoyment and suffering, the lives of all people involve, or have, both intrinsic goodness and intrinsic evil. If the amounts of each were somehow fixed and unchanging so that nothing could be done about a person's fate, then there would be no need for ethics, or, for that matter, the sciences or any of the efforts put forth to improve supplies of goods and services or to motivate attitudes and desires. Ethics, as we shall see, is concerned with how to maximize the intrinsic goodness of life. Concerns for increasing enjoyments in particular areas, such as economics, politics, marriage, recreation, education, etc., can be called economic ethics, political ethics, marital ethics, etc. But when one becomes concerned about the enjoyment of his life as a whole, we call this comprehensive area "religious ethics"; endeavors relative to thinking through the nature of life as a whole and how it may best achieve the most in the way of goodness for it are properly called "philosophical."

We cannot examine here diversities among philosophies about the nature of life, nor the doctrines and practices designed to accomplish the ends of life so differently conceived. But all must somehow conceive the intrinsic value of a life as more than momentary. Otherwise the "live for the moment" spirit would prevail and reckless impulses, whether motivated by fear or greed, would shorten lives and thereby decrease their total intrinsic value. If life is good, i.e. has a significant surplus of enjoyment over suffering, then a long life is better. If maintenance of enjoyable life depends upon availability and wise ultilization of potential instrumental values, concern for such values is basic to religion. This is why in times when life itself is threatened—as when a person is about to die or when a whole people is endangered by famine, epidemic or war—people call upon religious specialists for guidance. People who experience comfort from such guidance tend to want to keep such specialists available as potential instrumental values. The more fearful people become about threats to life as a whole, the more importance they attach to religious matters, regardless of whether they share or repudiate the locally orthodox views.

If feelings are momentary, and if there are times when our feelings are neutral rather than good or bad and times when we apparently have no conscious feelings, as in a dreamless sleep, does a life then have no intrinsic value? Our answer has to be yes; but because a life has potential for reawakening its feelings, it has potential intrinsic value. And here, doubtless, is the most important reason why potential intrinsic values are important, and why it is important to want to keep alive and to want others to continue to live. Hence, so far as future enjoyment of life is concerned, potential intrinsic values are all-important.

The conditions which make life possible, e.g. biological and physiological, behave as conditional potential values; so long as we have and are aware of having any control over them, they serve as bases for conditional oughts. It is because a person has potentialities for future enjoyments that he has an obligation to live; and because he has potentialities for improving his potentialities for greater enjoyment in life, he has obligations to "realize his potentialities" or to "make the most of his life." Any believed means for maintaining or increasing the intrinsic value of one's life as a whole becomes for him his most important potential instrumental value. And, to the extent that it is possible to generalize about the bases for such beliefs, it becomes desirable to work out some scheme as to which potential instruments promise to yield the greatest value. An adequate science of ethics will investigate and reach tentative conclusions regarding probable heirarchies of relatively higher and lower, i.e. promising greater or lesser, potential intrinsic values.

Instrumental Value of Life

The potential intrinsic values of a life depend for their existence upon the potential instrumental values which can cause them. Hence, in improving health, or maintaining the life of a body, we are more directly concerned with instrumental values. All of a person's capacities—including mental, moral, economic, social and political—behave as instrumentalities having power to induce and maintain intrinsic values. We have already presupposed in the foregoing that the potentially intrinsic depend upon the potentially instrumental, so merely mention here that the focus of attention of our ethical endeavors appropriately tends to be upon ourselves as instrumental values.

But, especially in our dealing with others, we so often enjoy results of utilizing others for our purposes that we sometimes forget to recognize that maximization of their intrinsic values is also essential to ethical endeavor. This tendency to forget or to disregard the intrinsic values, potential as well as actual, of others has led many moralists to produce maxims to remind us. Perhaps the most-quoted formula is that of the extreme rationalist, Immanuel Kant, who gives the name, "categorical imperative," to the command to "treat humanity, whether in yourself or others, always as an end, and never as a means merely."

PART III
ETHICS

CHAPTER 6

OUGHTS OR OBLIGATIONS

What Is "Oughtness"?

"OUGHTNESS" CONSISTS in the power which an apparently greater good has over an apparently lesser good, or which an apparently lesser evil has over an apparently greater evil, in compelling our choices. Why ought one choose a greater good in preference to a lesser good? Just because it is greater. Since intrinsic values are the ultimate values, they are the ultimate sources of our duties and obligations. But since intrinsic values depend upon the instrumental value of whatever brings them into existence, many, if not most, of our decisions pertain to instrumental values. When so, the apparent greater probability that one kind of action, or behavior, will result in greater intrinsic value than another itself functions as the deciding factor for our feeling of obligation. All other, more specific meanings of "oughtness" and "obligation," which are synonyms for present purposes, derive form this general basis.

"Oughtness" exists actually only when one faces alternatives. If, for any reason or any period of time, a person has no alternatives, either because he has achieved his goals and occupies himself entirely with enjoying them or because he finds himself so situated that he is completely helpless, he has no obligations. Such situations are extremely rare, for even in the absence of other obligations, one may have an obligation to choose between being willing or unwilling to be resigned to his situation. Hence, whenever one becomes aware of alternative values calling for his decision in choosing between them, a feeling of oughtness emerges with such awareness. The intensity of such feelings tend to vary with the believed greatness of the values at stake, though at times such intensity results also from feelings of provocation at the difficulties felt in trying to reach a decision.

"Oughtness" also exists only in the presence of volition or intention. Conscious choice involves intending to choose. And intending to choose occurs, presumably, only when one is conscious. Since both volition or intention and consciousness vary in degrees, i.e. one may be more or less conscious and more or less intending, we are, in attempting to understand the nature of obligation, plunged immediately into a whole host of problems. This introductory treatment of ethics as a science is no place for long treatises on the nature and conditions of consciousness, intention, freedom of will or choosing. But some recognition of the kinds and complexity of problems involved in understanding obligation is needed. We shall first summarize some of the ways in which all oughts or feelings of obligation are alike, and then survey a few of the problems which continue to provoke dispute in the absence of sustained scientific effort to deal with them. (This survey suggests additional reasons why development of ethics as a science has been neglected and additional areas in which further substantial research is needed. It will show, too, that many of the difficulties stem from the fact that definitive solutions await completion of unfinished work in other sciences.)

Essential Conditions of Oughtness

Essential conditions of the existence of oughtness, i.e. ways in which all ethical situations are alike, include the following:

1. All are experienced, or depend upon awareness or conscious for their actual existence.

2. All involve values, and the ways in which all value situations are alike, as discussed in Part I, including both intrinsic and instrumental values, potential and actual values, and experiencing values as objects.

3. All involve facing choices between alternatives.

4. All involve volition or intention.

5. All involve feelings, for all actual obligations are, or involve, feelings of obligation.

6. All are intuited or directly apprehended because all feelings are intuited or directly apprehended.

7. All are subjective in the sense that they are, or involve, feelings. Furthermore, all are subjective in the sense that all of the ideas in terms of which obligations are conceived also occur in consciousness.

8. All involve conceptualization. Although there may be times when one feels that he ought to do something without knowing quite what it is that he ought to do, he can hardly feel that he has obligation in the full sense until he begins to become clear about what he ought to do. That is, one may believe that he has obligations which he is unclear about, but may also feel uncertain about what his obligations are and how much he is obligated so long as lack of clarity in conception and lack of assurance regarding his understanding of the issues at stake remain. Hence development of conceptions, clarity of conceptions and assurance that conceptions are relatively adequate all appear to be involved in the nature of obligation or oughtness.

9. All involve objectification of ideas; i.e. about what one's alternatives are, about what his obligation is, about what course of action or inaction should be taken, and about what kinds of consequences may be expected. If one has reified his ideas of values at stake, then he is more likely to reify also his conception of his obligation. He may say to himself, "I really do have this obligation even though I wish I didn't have it." Refication is more likely when others are involved and when one believes that others share his conception of what his obligation is. Understanding obligation involves all of those problems previously summarized in discussing naive, scientific and pragmatic realistic theories of knowledge. Among the problems pressing persons responsible for guiding others is how to prevent persons from being too naively realistic about their obligations and then, after discovering essentially subjective aspects of obligations, from shifting too completely to a view that obligations are purely subjective, completely arbitrary, or foolish illusions. Maintenance of a pragmatic attitude toward finding out how much both subjective and real factors condition each particular obligation seems called for. Awareness

both that one's ideas and feelings about his obligations behave, and that they are better understood and managed when one treats them as behavioral processes, may enable one to make more fitting adjustments to both his internal and external problems.

10. All are forward-looking. Actual obligations always involve present feelings, but they are conceived in such a way that present decisions will have future consequences. One may now believe that he ought to have done differently in the past; and he may now believe that he ought to make restitution for a past mistake. He may, therefore, now believe that he did in the past have an obligation which he did not fulfill; but this results from his reification of his ideas about obligation which can be reified as if past, present or future. One may now believe that by deciding now to marry, for example, he will have future obligations, some of which he may and some of which he may not now know. But regardless of whether or how reified, expectation of future consequences, no matter how unclearly conceived, seem to be implicit in every feeling of oughtness. (The significance of consequences is sufficiently great that some theorists have defined rightness and wrongness of action entirely in terms of consequences, ignoring or denying the role of intentions. This is a mistake, I believe; but how it can occur when people not only conceive obligations in terms of intended consequences but also normally naively reify their conceptions in terms of the consequences anticipated is understandable.)

11. All involve feelings of compulsion. The power involved is not physical, though uncritical minds may fail to distinguish one kind of compulsion from another, and those unfortunate enough to have acquired their views about the nature of obligation from childhood spankings may habitually regard the compulsion experienced in feelings of obligation as akin to or not much different from those experienced when physical force is applied to prod or prevent their action. Unfortunately, also, the frequency with which negative commands and corporal punishments condition early experiences of obligation cause some to conceive obligations wholly in negative terms. "Stop this." "Don't do that." "That's wrong." "You ought not . . .!" Our analysis of the ultimate locus of the compulsory power felt as oughtness points to intrinsic values, both

enjoyments and suffering; and although further studies may show that suffering more often or more effectively motivates feelings of obligation than enjoyments, I believe that a science of ethics will prove more serviceable if theories are worked out in terms of positive values or, better, both positive and negative values, than if negative values are stressed as primary. Surely students will be more willing to approach the subject more rationally if appeals are made to positive, or both positive and negative, values than if appeals are made in ways such that childhood fears and ruthless environments prejudicially inhibit relatively objective approaches.

12. All involve feelings of agency. Will or intention, already mentioned, involves accepting one's self as an agent or actor. Unfortunately, some who approach ethics as a science regard its subject matter as mores, and therefore as a branch of anthropology, and study ethical behavior in terms of conformity or nonconformity to customary behavior patterns. The commonness or peculiarity of such behavior patterns are taken as the primary substance being investigated. But moral action from the viewpoint of the actor involves problems, choices, decisions and actions not only in which his own welfare is at stake but for which he is the actor, i.e. the chooser, the decider, the executer. Accepting oneself as an agent presupposes accepting oneself as existing, and some conception of self. Such conception may be vague or clear, simple or complex, and of oneself as rigid or flexible.

How one comes to conceive himself is a subject already profusely described, but also one needing further research. An infant somehow discovers himself behaving as an actor, and presumably biological needs for survival conditioned developments in men and other animals to act, and to learn about themselves as actors, by how they find themselves behaving in various situations in which action is aroused. Some may believe that when a body produces sufficient energy so that muscles become activated, the need for self awareness emerged. George Herbert Mead has contributed the view that ideas of self as actor arise when and because one finds himself treated as an object by others and that then he responds or reacts to stimuli from others. By reacting to such stimuli, one thereby acts; he can then observe how his action affects others and how their reactions again in turn affect him and how he reacts again. Discovery of self as actor is a great adventure, and later, when one has mastered the art of self-control, one may plan new experiments in self-discovery and, indeed, self-development. Habits of self-conception may become fixed and rigid; they may emphasize self as patient, with consequent tendencies toward fear or self-pity and reluctance to act or to act vigorously or decisively; they may burgeon into self as dauntless, as powerful, as proud or as commanding. Problems of ego formation and malformation investigated by depth psychologists have bearings upon the ways in which people conceive and accept themselves as agents, and, hence, how they conceive and accept themselves as obligated. The behavior of selves as agents is an observable phenomenon, both externally and, for those who have developed sufficient critical abilities, introspectively. And correlations between variations in self-conceptions and conceptions of oughtness doubtless also are observable.

Agency connotes power to initiate. An act of will involves some notion of self-activity. No matter what theory of causation one accepts—i.e. whether will is causally determined completely, is completely uncaused or is partially uncaused—a feeling of agency as self-activity seems a necessary condition to experiencing feelings of oughtness. A person in catatonia or deep sleep is not regarded as an agent, and surely has no actual oughtness, no matter what his potentialities.

13. All involve feelings of commitment. Such commitment is of two sorts, namely, to choose or decide and to act on one's decision or to carry out one's intentions. The distinction between them may not arise in awareness, especially when need for instant decision and action is called for. At other times, the distinction not only is clear but performance of the two functions becomes widely separated, as when governments establish separate legislative and administrative branches for the special purposes of choosing among alternatives and reaching policy decisions to which the state thereby commits itself, on the one hand, and of putting into practice, sometimes through laborious, lasting and costly efforts, the decisions reached, on the other.

The commitments involved in feelings of obligation vary greatly.

They may arise and subside in a moment of anger, or they may be long in forming, as in choosing a career, and may be long in execution, as when marriage contracts require intention to continue "until death do us part" or even "throughout time and eternity." They may pertain to trivial issues, as when deciding to move right or left in a checker game, or to one's whole life, as in an oath of allegiance when joining military service. They may be extremely general, as when a college dean or president agrees to be responsible for whatever unforeseen situations call for, or extremely limited, as when insurance contracts stipulate precise conditions for liability and exact amounts of payments due. They may function as implicit in one's behavior, as when approaching another without hostile warning conveys intention not to harm, or they may require strict conformity to preestablished ritual, as when a president takes an oath of office or when a "last will and testament" requires formal signature by a notary public before witnesses who can testify that the signer is "in full possession of his mental powers." They may occur as highly conditional, e.g. "If Mary gets here in time and has enough money, then we will go to the movie if Walt Disney's 'Bambi' is on," or utterly unconditional, "I will see to it that your Dad gets you a bicycle, even if I have to pay for it myself."

Notice that commitment to carry out decisions over a period of time involves a commitment to future commitments, since as time goes on one may face on each new relevant occasion the problem of whether to continue to carry out the previous commitment. Some commitments are regarded as irrevocable and hence as precommitting all future choices. Others are regarded as contingent in the sense that, although no change in policy is intended, if unforseen circumstances prevent carrying out the decision, then a new decision must be reached about what modifications in the commitment are required and/or permissible. Long-range personal commitments, i.e. of the sort involved when a person decides to live his life in a certain way, then behave as character traits; and since some kinds of commitments are essential for certain kinds of professions, we are sometimes able to judge something about the nature of a person's commitments and conceptions of his obligations by the kind of profession in which he is engaged. Furthermore, whatever else conscience is, a continuing feeling of obligation to carry out a commitment is often spoken of as "conscience" and a person who tries to fulfill his obligations fully as "conscientious."

14. All involve potentiality as well as actuality. I do not assert that the actuality-potentiality distinction must be kept clearly in mind while one is having feelings of obligation. But since what is actual could not have become actual unless there existed that which brought it into existence, and since what is actual will cause other actualities to become, each actuality, including each actual obligation, involves potentiality in these two senses. Awareness of the distinction is important because when we talk about obligations, especially other people's obligations, most of our judgments will be found to refer to potentialities, or the actualization of potentialities, if we stop to examine the matter carefully. In order to suggest the magnitude of such importance, we will sketch a few of the difficulties involved. We find here another nest of problems which constantly cause confusion in ethical thinking.

a. The word "potentiality" has several meanings. Confusion here causes confusion elsewhere. Two main types of these meanings may be clarified by citing an example. So let us suppose that we are looking at an oak tree, which, being present, is actual, and someone refers to "its potentiality." What does he mean?

(1) Sometimes one intends to refer to the power or powers which brought it into being. The existence of our present oak tree had many causes, including an acorn, nutrient soil, moisture, sunshine, time to germinate, grow and mature, freedom from competing or destructive forces, and many more. All of these together contributed causally to bringing our present oak tree into actual existence. All of these together, thus, were "its potentiality" in our first meaning of the term. If any one of the causes needed for its coming into being had been missing, it would not have come into being. Hence, the actual oak tree depended upon all of "its potentialities," in this sense, in order to become the actual oak tree which it is. No one of the causes alone, and no collection of the causes from which one of the needed causes was missing, could have caused it to be actual. Each of such causes is then called a

"conditional potentiality." Each has the power to produce the oak tree only if all of the other causes cooperate in contributing their power.

Turning from our particular tree to tree science, we observe that some kinds of conditional potentialities are more significant than others in the growth of oak trees. First of all, oak tree growth requires an acorn and not a chestnut. Since biological beings exist in species, each of which requires its own kind of seed or specific source as a conditional potentiality, convenience dictates that we speak as if the potentiality of the oak tree exists already in the acorn. The conditions for its genetic type do exist. But these are not sufficient. Other kinds of needed conditions have limitations also, for the moisture needed must be water, not gasoline. The sunshine must not be too hot. Many variations in each of the kinds of conditional potentialities needed can be observed, but limitations upon such variations are also required. An ideally adequate tree science should be able to tell us both all of the kinds of conditional potentialities needed for each kind of tree together with the range of variations permissable. But our particular actually existing oak tree did have all of the needed particular conditional potentialities each with its particular place on such range, so to speak; and all of these particular conditional potentialities together are "its" potentialities, in our first meaning of the term.

(2) Sometimes we become interested in making a table out of an oak tree, and then, to the extent that the oak tree is such that it can be made into a table, we can say that it has the potentiality of becoming a table, meaning that it has a conditional potentiality if all other needed conditional potentialities—such as the desire to make it into a table, a carpenter, a plan, the work of cutting, sawing, planing, sanding, etc.—cooperate. But if, as I cut down the tree, my wife persuades me we need some chairs more than a table, then the tree's potentiality for becoming chairs is noted. We can recognize that our oak tree has many conditional potentialities, including being made into a beam, a wagon tongue, a bridge, a flag pole, paper pulp and firewood. In our second sense, all of these and more are "its potentialities," all of which are also conditional potentialities in our second meaning of the term.

Confusion of the two foregoing meanings is confounded by the prevalence of inadequate and conflicting views about the relative fixity of hereditarily determined biological potentialities. Ideas at least as old as Aristotle depict "the potentiality" of our oak tree as not only essentially fixed and unchanging but already wholly present in its antecedent acorn, and the same essence recurring, fixed and complete, in each acorn which it produces. Hence, in a sense exactly the same potentiality regarded as real—i.e. existing whether we know it or not—occurs first in an acorn, which is then actualized fully in a mature oak tree, and then recurs in each of the acorns which it produces. Current biochemical studies penetrate more deeply into how apparent abnormalities in development result from the ways in which variations in chromosome structure program differently an individual's growth.

Although it is still true that oak trees can grow only from acorns and not from chestnuts, for example, notions of hereditary species as much less fixed, and of the nature of biological potentialities as much more dynamic, have replaced those inherited from Aristotle. We cannot here explore the intricate issues in either the metaphysical or biological potentiality-actuality problems; but we must note that, to the extent that reliable conclusions in ethics as a science relative to conditional and actual oughts depend upon solution of potentiality-actuality problems in metaphysics and biology, ethicists have vested interests in having those problems solved soon. To the extent that clarity in ethics depends upon clarity in biology and metaphysics, failure to have dealt adequately with the relevant problems in these fields naturally contributes to the lack of adequacy in ethical theory; but too many people falsely believe that such failure in ethical theory is peculiar to it and cannot be resolved while at the same time having faith that such failures in biology and metaphysics are merely temporary. Part of the difficulty in understanding both conditional and actual oughts lies in failures to understand the relatively dynamic nature of, and omnipresent multiplicities of, conditional potentialities—metaphysical, biological, etc., as well as ethical. But once the complicated interrelatedness between the conditional potentialities dealt with in ethics and all other sciences is recognized, then needed research into such interrelations can be undertaken and substantial progress in further understanding the ways in which conditional oughts depend upon conditional potentialities can be expected.

   b. The word "actual" also has several meanings.

   (1) Metaphysically, "actual" means existing now. Difficulties arise, however, as soon as we examine the meaning of "now" or "present," since the many different theories of time prevailing interpret "the present" differently. Some say that the present has only an infinitesimal duration whereas others speak of the present moment, present hour, present day, present month, present year and present century. Without examining these difficulties here, we can say that whatever kind of duration an actual feeling of obligation has is something with which any adequate physical or metaphysical theory of time must come to terms. Too often theories designed to account for problems in one area of experience, once accepted, are used to deny the existence of data serving as evidence for theories in other areas of experience. An adequate philosophy, i.e. one in which both metaphysical and ethical phenomena are both adequately and consistently accounted for, cannot use conclusions drawn from one kind of data to deny the existence of other kinds of existing data. Another kind of metaphysical difficulty has to do with proper verbal accounting for how now-existing conditional potentialities are at once actual in the sense of now existing, and potential in the sense that they are potentialities for future existences. The point I am stressing is not that these difficulties cannot be overcome, but that they appear as difficulties in ethical theory because they exist as difficulties in metaphysical theory (and hence also in physics, mathematics, chemistry, biology, etc.).

   (2) Psychologically, "actual" means present in awareness. Ignoring other meanings of the term used by psychologists, we select this meaning to emphasize that, since oughtness or obligation depends upon awareness or consciousness for its actual existence (see the first essential condition), it does not exist actually apart from such awareness. Hence, even though all of the other conditions for the existence of such awareness of oughtness may be actual, if awareness is essential to the actualization of oughtness,

actual oughtness does not exist in the absence of actual awareness. Problems here are complicated by the fact that sometimes we are drowsy, or only half-awake, and that we may, during a period of several moments or hours, vary greatly in the degrees of alertness and thus, in a sense, in degrees of awakeness. Those who believe that oughtness and rightness should rest on more substantial bases than variations in drowsiness will resist, if not reject outright, this condition of oughtness and this conception of the actuality of particular oughts. But if they keep in mind that the rigor they demand can and must be accounted for primarily in terms of conditional potentialities, the seeming difficulties will not be so great. They indicate the importance of attention to alertness and to preparations for maintaining alertness in situations where important obligations are at stake; and they indicate the importance of these conditional potentialities, called "habits," "character traits" or "virtues," which are established tendencies to act, even spontaneously, in certain types of critical situations.

(3) The word "actual" may be used to denote the presence, in a person, of developed habits, character traits or virtues (i.e. strengths or capacities), regardless of whether they are functioning in actual awareness. That is, if one person has developed the ability to drive carefully and another has not, then the one has actual habits, character traits or virtues which the other does not have. However, since while a careful driver is not actually driving, such habits are not actually functioning, there is a sense in which, although existing as conditional potentialities, they do so actually exist in ways in which an untrained driver's conditional potentialities do not.

(4) A somewhat similar meaning of the word "actual" is relevant in cases where one has interests of which he is unaware. These may be stated in conditional or subjective modes of expression. For example, we may observe a person suddenly angered in a situation where his life is at stake. The immediate evils overwhelm his consciousness and he strongly experiences an actual ought to retaliate. But, we observe, if he could be aware of all of the other values which will be actualized if he lives, then he would choose not to risk his life in a moment of anger. Which are his

"actual" interests, those of which he is aware at the moment or those consisting of his conditional potentialities for many more actual enjoyments in the future of which he is not now aware? Strictly speaking, only those of which he is aware are "actual" in sense (2) above. Yet there is also a very fundamental sense in which concern for actualizing conditional potentialities which will yield the greatest enjoying of intrinsic value during a lifetime is one's greatest ought. Many find it difficult not to speak of such conditional potentialities as in some sense actual, for we often find ourselves inclined to say: "Actually he should have controlled his anger so that he would not have been killed." We say that a person is "beside himself," or is "temporarily insane," when he sacrifices opportunities for actualizing great intrinsic value for immediate goals which overwhelm his consciousness.

(5) Yet, the word "actual" applies most properly to oughtness only while one is actually experiencing a feeling of obligation. One may be actually aware of a problem, of the alternatives at stake, of the apparently superior values of one of the alternatives, and yet, if, for some reason, no feeling of obligation arises in his awareness, then we can hardly say that he actually has a feeling of obligation. Actual oughtness does not exist until oughtness actually exists, to state the matter tautologically. Our impatience with the seeming triviality of such an absolutistic statement should indicate that although on the one hand, since actual oughtness exists ultimately only in this way, we should be most concerned about it, on the other hand, since most of our oughts and most of our control over the conditions of oughtness pertain to potential oughts, most of our concern both as ethical scientists and as particular persons should be with conditional oughts. It is true that we can easily become lost in a vast sea of conditional oughts; but if we desire to achieve richer rewards, we ought to give more attention to navigation.

c. Generalizations about what people ought to do under certain kinds of circumstances seem irresistible when we observe that similar kinds of situations recur and when we find that social survival often depends upon people acting in similar ways in similar situations. The following hypothesis, for example, seems obviously true. If, in a situation conditioned by a given set of circumstances (i.e. conditional oughts), and if one actually ought to act in a particular way, then if an exactly similar situation with exactly the same kinds of circumstances recurs, then one ought also to act in that same way. But also, to one who is aware of the almost endless varieties of intricately different sets of circumstances, the likelihood that two situations will ever be exactly the same is remote. Yet empirical studies of similarities in ethical situations can provide bases for useful generalizations.

For example, data about relationships between accident rates at street crossings and amount and speed of traffic are now already well known, and empirical studies of accident rates at particular street crossings have been made. Although decisions are based upon probabilities, i.e. about conditional oughts, experienced traffic managers use statistical data as bases for erecting stop signs and, until conditions change, usually are satisfied that they "have done what they ought." Furthermore, experience with the costliness of failures to develop and practice habits of coming to a full stop at stop signs, even if only on the basis of statistical probabilities, causes us to believe that, as a matter of moral practice, we ought to enforce practice of such habits at all times. Regulations based on experiences with actualizing conditional potentialities have proved worthwhile, and such worthiness is sufficient basis for continuing their practice. The role of statistics in reaching decisions about how to act in multitudes of kinds of situations has already been widely accepted. But neglect to accept such role as an important part of the way in which conditional oughts are determined has characterized ethical theory. An adequate science of ethics will make great use of statistical data, and increasingly make use of computerized technology in assembling and generalizing about such data. Difficulties inherent in theories of probability, gathering and interpreting statistics and the use and misuse of computers all become difficulties inherent in ethical theory and practice. Here again, however, many of the difficulties can be seen to exist in ethics because they exist as difficulties in other sciences.

Being able to locate such difficulties does not thereby clear up confusion. Awareness of the kinds of difficulties involved in the presence of both the actuality and potentiality involved in the existence of oughtness helps us to realize that knowing that both actuality and potentiality are common to all ethical situations does not immediately yield clarity; but it does make clear that such likenesses do provide bases for developing ethics as a very complicated science.

What Is Intention, Volition or Will?

Ignoring distinctions between these three words which may be found useful, we focus attention upon two of the many problems which must be dealt with by an adequate science of ethics: (1) freedom of will and (2) degrees of intention.

1. Acts are right or wrong only if voluntary. Oughtness exists actually only when acts are intentional. One's acts are his own only when and if he freely chooses to act. Hence some workable solution of the problem of the nature of will is essential to a workable science of ethics. A crucial question is often stated: "Is the will free?" When so stated, attention is more often directed to the meaning of "freedom" than to the meaning of "will." Much ink has been spilled in disputations about the meaning of "freedom," and at least six different theories continue to receive support by adherents: Freedom consists in (1) absence of restraint (some say only external restraint, others include internal restraint), (2) indeterminism, (3) self-determinism, (4) fitness of capacities and opportunities, (5) submission of lower to higher values (includes theistic, rationalistic, romanticistic, Vedantic, Taoistic and Organicistic varieties), (6) acceptance of self as agent or originator of action, and various combinations of these six.*

My study of these and other theories of freedom of will has resulted in a generalization about them and the formulation of a generic theory: Freedom consists in the ability to do what you want to do. The foregoing theories do not disagree that this is at least a part of what they mean by "freedom," but they differ regarding the nature of abilities and wants.

The most disputed theory—namely, that a thing, self or will is

---

*For details, see Archie J. Bahm, Self as free. *Why Be Moral?* (Publication projected), Ch. 10.

free only when it is uncaused or undetermined—sharply divides
proponents into two utterly opposing camps. One of these claims
that, since nothing exists without a cause, everything is determined,
and hence there is no freedom. The other claims that, since freedom
of will is directly experienced, either nothing is caused or determined (a view not widely held) or there are two kinds of beings,
those which are caused or determined and those which are uncaused or free. The crux of the issue is that both sides accept
determined and undetermined, or unfree and free, as divided by
an excluded middle. Aristotle's principle of excluded middle was
called a "law of thought," i.e. one seeking clarity in his conceptions about classes of objects needs to be able to distinguish conceptions so sharply that different kinds will have no members in
common. But, unwittingly, too many hastily conclude that a "law
of thought" is also a "law of reality," and that, by a mere act of
thought, whenever one uses the word "not" (logicians symbolize
this by A and not-A), he can split the existing universe (logicians
speak rather of a "universe of discourse") into two separate and
unrelated parts. Nothing can be both free and unfree in the same
sense at the same time. But cooler heads have discovered that
"freedom" and "determinism" may characterize the same thing,
including will, in two different senses at the same time. Aspect
logics better explain some aspects of experience than do class logics.

Details of this issue cannot be explored here. I wish only to call
attention to certain points.

a. The issue is primarily one of the nature of logic and metaphysics, not primarily one in ethics as a science merely as such;
that is, any failure here is a failure on the part of metaphysicians
and logicians, upon whom ethicists depend, and pertains to inadequacies in logic as a science and metaphysics (including physics)
as a science. The popular presumptions that logic and physics have
completed their work as sciences and that ethics as a science can
never complete its work are both false. Some present inadequacies
in ethics as a science may also result in inadequacies in logic and
physics as sciences.

b. The rise of Emergentism as a distinct type of philosophy,*

---

*See Archie J. Bahm, *Philosophy, An Introduction* (Bombay, Asia, 1964), Ch. 18.

itself a much-neglected Copernican revolution, and its successors—
Creationism and Organicism[†]—opened the way for multi-level conceptions of causation and the perpetual emergence of novelty in
casual processes. It also provided a refutation to the claim that
the view that "nothing happens without a cause necessarily implies
that there can be no freedom."[‡]

c. Further research in both logic and metaphysics is needed
and those interested in developing ethics as a science should also
be interested in such research, especially to the extent that it has
implications for ethics.

d. My generic theory can serve as a workable theory even in
the absence of additional agreement about other issues. For the
theory that "freedom of will consists in being able to do what you
want to do," which is both intuitively obvious and remains completely ambiguous relative to the determinism-indeterminism issue,
cannot only serve as a working hypothesis but must also be incorporated, implicitly at least, in any other theory demanding additional essential specifications. That is, this theory says nothing
about whether either one's wants or one's abilities are determined or
indetermined. Hence, as a generic form, it is compatible with both
the deterministic and the indeterministic specifications.

2. Our second problem, much more serious even if much less
debated, pertains to degrees of volition or degrees of intention.
I am not suggesting that any meter can be devised for measuring
degree of intention; but it is obvious that sometimes we will more
strongly than at others, choose more decisively than at others or
intend more fully than at others. The issue is significant to the
extent that variations in intention involve variations in actual oughtness (or degrees of intention determine degrees of oughtness) and
to the extent that variations in feelings of responsibility depend
upon variations in intention. Hence, an adequate ethical theory
will recognize and explain the relationships and variations involved.

We propose, here, not to settle the issue but merely to raise
some questions which call for solution. Are actions always either

---

[†]*Ibid.*, Chs. 19 and 20.

[‡]Archie J. Bahm, The freedom-determinism controversy. Originally published in *The
Pakistan Philosophical Journal*, 9(3):48-55, Jan. 1965. To be published in *Why Be
Moral?* Ch. 10.

intended or unintended exclusively, or may they be partly intended and partly unintended? Sometimes we intend to act but do not, by such action, intend to produce certain unforseen consequences. An officer may enforce a policy of which he does not as a person approve; to the extent that he does not approve it, he may not intend the consequences. To what extent is "permissive intent," where we intend not to intend, different from "insistent intent," where we intend to intend to influence the course of events? Do we have subconscious intentions? When we feel forced to act even when uncertain about what consequences will follow, to what extent are we intending the consequences which actually occur? When variations in energy, from extreme weakness when ill to extreme intensity when vigorous and enthusiastic, produce differences in the intensity with which we feel our intentions, do they thereby cause differences in degrees of oughtness? Does intention fully exist as soon as we intend to act even though we do not act, or when we begin an action which we do not continue, or when we continue an action up to the last phase without finishing it, or only when we have finished it completely?*

---

*For further details see *Why Be Moral?* Ch. 9.

CHAPTER 7

SOME PRINCIPLES FOR CHOOSING*

To THE EXTENT THAT persons and their circumstances are alike, bases for generalization exist. The purpose of the present chapter is to state and examine some of the very general principles for choosing between values. These principles may vary in degree of obviousness. The universality of their applicability may be tested by different persons with varying degrees of success. Hence, they are proposed here as hypotheses. To the writer, they seem both intuitively obvious and testable without exception. They will be arranged for convenience into six groups.

Principles Applying to Both Intrinsic and Instrumental Values

Our first general principle is that, other things being equal, when faced with a choice between two alternatives, one of which is good and the other evil, a person ought always to choose the good alternative. The principle consists in the good (ultimately, the intrinsic good) being the ultimate locus of power for compelling our choices.

The phrase, "other things being equal," applies not only to the principle under consideration here but to all the principles for choosing proposed in this article.

A second general principle pertains to alternatives consisting in greater and lesser goods and to alternatives consisting in greater and lesser evils. This will be considered in three aspects. The first aspect may be stated as follows: When faced with the problem of choosing between two alternatives, one of which is good and the other better, other things being equal, one ought always to choose

---

*The contents of this chapter appeared first in *Philosophy Today,* 9:52-60, Spring 1965.

the better. The second aspect may be stated as follows: When faced with the problem of choosing between two alternatives, one of which is bad and the other worse, other things being equal, one ought always to choose the bad rather than the worse. The third aspect, which combines and extends the first two aspects, may be stated as follows: When faced with the problem of choosing between two or more alternatives, some of which are better than others and some of which are worse than others, other things being equal, one ought always to choose the most good and least evil possible.

These three aspects have their explanation in the general principle that of two goods (ultimately, two intrinsic goods) one of which is better than the other, the greater goodness of the one has within itself the power to compel our will to choose it, and that of two evils (ultimately, two intrinsic evils), one of which is worse than the other, the greater evil of the one has within itself the power to compel our will to choose to avoid it.

We might, at this point, note that the first principle stated above has been incorporated into the statement of the third aspect. The inclusion of simpler principles in more complex principles does not eliminate them, though it may eliminate need for enumerating them. Rather such inclusion indicates not only that complex principles depend upon simpler ones but also that simpler ones which exist as statements based on partial similarities between situations involve, and are involved in, the more complex principles needed to complete their own nature and contribution to an interpretation and codification of general principles for choosing which is adequate to account for the more complex similarities existing between situations.

Principles Pertaining Primarily to Intrinsic Values

The options confronted with respect to the problem of choosing among alternative intrinsic values (a problem which does not arise to one wholly immersed in enjoyment of intrinsic value) have to do with actualizing potential intrinsic values or with more fully appreciating intrinsic values only partly actualized. To the extent that all intrinsic values may be experienced as "enjoyments"—such as feelings of pleasure, enthusiasm, satisfaction, contentment, or any blending of these (see Chapter 3)—rules for choosing can be formulated.

To the extent that enjoyments differ in "quantity," when faced with the problem of choosing between greater or lesser quantity, other things being equal, one ought always choose the greater quantity. If they differ in "duration," when faced with the problem of choosing between longer or shorter durations of an enjoyment, other things being equal, one ought always choose the longer-lasting enjoyment. Where they differ in "intensity," when faced with the problem of choosing between a more intense and a less intense enjoyment, other things being equal, one ought always choose the more intense enjoyment. When they differ in "quality," when faced with the problem of choosing between a higher quality and a lower quality enjoyment, other things being equal, one ought always choose the higher quality enjoyment.

Now since, during a particular period in which prospective enjoyments are to be experienced, they may have both quantitative, durational, intensive and qualitative aspects, the issue normally becomes one of whether to choose quantity versus duration, duration versus intensity, intensity versus quality, quantity versus quality, duration versus quality, quantity versus intensity or, rather, between more complex (e.g. quantity-intensity versus duration-quality) alternatives. Since situations normally also contain awareness of objects or object-complexes and activities or activity-complexes, choice-problems regarding the above-outlined alternatives seldom appear so sharply defined. Vagueness, uncertainty, even ignorance, regarding such issues leave us usually victims of whim, impulse or inclination. Nevertheless, the foregoing principles for choosing among enjoyments should appear, upon reflection, as naturally reasonable conditional oughts. Although "other things" are seldom if ever equal, awareness of the availability of such principles may provide both additional assurance (and enjoyment in being a person who can, if he chooses, choose on principle, which enjoyment itself may be experienced as an intrinsic value) and actual assistance whenever issues do occur in sharpened form. The principles are significant also because they carry over into decisions regarding the making of instruments. Ought we manufacture instruments which produce more quantity, duration, intensity or quality of pleasures? These principles bear also upon how we feel we ought to treat our friends, for we might rightly choose to tickle a child, praise a youth, evidence fidelity to a spouse, and sit quietly conversing about life with an oldster, whereas reversing such options could have quite different effects.

The foregoing principles for choosing pertaining primarily to intrinsic values presuppose as self-evident the principle that intrinsic value is its own "reason for being." A thing which is an end in itself requires no other "reason for being," no other teleological explanation, even though its causal, conditional and compositional explanation may be infinitely complex and necessarily uncertain. To the extent that anything is an end in itself, it ought to be appreciated, whenever one is faced with the alternative of whether to appreciate or not to appreciate it and "other things" are "equal." If we remain unaware of things as ends in themselves or unaware of options concerning whether to appreciate them or not, they are beyond our opportunity or capacity for appreciation. But by becoming aware of intrinsic value as the ultimate locus of all value and of all obligation, and aware of our own ability to increase our appreciation of such value, we thereby become "more moral," more obligated and beings with more potential enjoyment of intrinsic value, than otherwise.

Principles Pertaining Primarily to Instrumental Values

First, since no enjoyment of intrinsic value can exist without life and since no life can exist without those instrumental causes and conditions essential to its nature, one needs to give attention to those instrumental values which are necessary to life. A general principle: When faced with the problem of choosing between means which are essential to life and means which are not essential to life, other things being equal, one ought to choose the means which are essential to life. The reason underlying this principle is that more intrinsic value will exist if life exists than if it does not exist. (If the life expected will be one of greater evil than of intrinsic good, however, then, other things being equal, one ought to choose means essential to ending such life.)

Secondly, by applying our "second general principle" cited above (i.e. other things being equal, one ought always to choose the most good and least evil possible) to problems pertaining primarily to choosing among instrumental values, we may note some typical kinds of issues relative to which we can state some typical subprinciples. Three of these will be noted: namely, those dealing with permanent versus transient instruments, those dealing with productive versus unproductive instruments and those dealing with efficient versus inefficient instruments.

1. When faced with the problem of choosing between two instruments—one of which is more enduring or more lasting as a potential instrumental value—other things being equal, one ought always to choose the more enduring in preference to the less enduring value.

2. When faced with the problem of choosing between two instruments—one of which is more productive in the sense that it is useful in producing more instruments which can produce still more instruments, etc., which function as potential instrumental values—other things being equal, one ought always to choose the more productive in preference to the less productive.

3. When faced with the problem of choosing between two instruments—one of which is more efficient in the sense that it produces, directly or indirectly, more intrinsic value than it involves intrinsic evil in its production, and the other of which is less efficient—other things being equal, one ought always to choose the former.

Regarding each of these three general subprinciples we may note that, although distinguishable, they are also similar in pertaining to more versus less instrumental value, in overlapping with respect to the instruments to which they apply, and in finding their justification in the common underlying principle which consists in one's long-range interests or in what is best for oneself in the long run, where "best for self in the long run" means greatest enjoyment of intrinsic value. Each is a form of the principle which Bentham called "fecundity." Each has a negative counterpart which together may be stated as a general code item: "Avoid waste." All may refer to instruments existing either outside or inside self; i.e.

to things existing external to self ("opportunities") and to character traits, habits, virtues ("capacities"); or to both ("abilities") and their fitness to each other. These three principles may be stated together as: When faced with the problem of choosing between two alternatives, one of which increases and the other of which decreases one's abilities in the long run, other things being equal, one ought always to choose the former. All may be involved in a shift in the ratio of significance of the permanent versus the transient, or the productive versus the unproductive, and the more versus the less efficient production as one's life proceeds; for if one has much life left to live, he may rightly be more concerned about enduring and productive goods than later in life—unless, and to the extent that, he expects himself to live on, in any of his levels of being, as identified with his children, his creations, his nation, his culture, mankind or ultimate reality itself.

We cannot reemphasize too often the significance of the phrase "other things being equal," for these principles may in actual application conflict with each other. For example, sometimes endurance (of delicately designed chinaware) should be preferred to efficiency (rapid washing of dishes), whereas at other times efficiency (in doing dishes with disposable paper or plastic dishes) should be preferred to endurance (involving washing, storing, protecting, repairing). Likewise, sometimes productive goods (machines for making machines) should be preferred to unproductive goods (machines for making decorations already in surplus), whereas at other times unproductive consumer's goods (food and clothing needed for survival) should be preferred to productive goods (machines for making machines whose products cannot be used until after the present generation of people is dead). The issue of whether to concentrate on production of "producers' goods versus consumers' goods," facing "underdeveloped nations" seeking rapid industrialization, is a matter of social policy which has its analogue in personal problems in which one constantly faces the issue of how much of his resources to spend in current fun and how much to save or invest for future safety.

Thirdly, another issue regarding instrumental values has to do with the relative certainty or uncertainty that a potential instrumental value will become actualized and result in actual enjoyment of intrinsic value. This issue is primarily "epistemological," i.e. concerned with knowledge, truth and certainty, rather than primarily "axiological," i.e. concerned with the nature of values. But it is axiological and ethical also to the extent that the rightness of one's choice in seeking to actualize the greatest amount of intrinsic value depends upon probabilities regarding prospects. Ethics, rightness, obligation and principles for choosing all depend upon epistemological conditions because such conditions are parts of the "other things" which may or may not be equal. Thus, "being moral involves not only "know thyself" in some adequate measure but also "know something about the nature of knowledge," including probability theory, and something about the nature of all the "other things" which may or may not be equal in relation to typical judging situations. The importance of knowing is part of "the importance of living."

This third issue may be formulated as follows: When faced with the problem of choosing between two instrumental values, one of which is more sure to result in an actual intrinsic value and the other of which is less sure, other things being equal, one ought always to choose the former. For example, a knife which is known to be sharp and sure to cut should be preferred to one which is dull and which may or may not cut, other things being equal. Or a brand of product which has always pleased should be chosen in preference to a new brand which is as yet untried, other things being equal. A kind of activity which has always yielded enjoyment should be favored against one which sometimes does and sometimes does not bring enjoyment. This issue and these examples have negative counterparts, of course. For example, a kind of activity which has always resulted in boredom should be avoided in preference to a kind of activity in which prospects regarding boredom remain uncertain, other things being equal.

Principles for Choosing Between Intrinsic and Instrumental Values

Three such general principles will be distinguished.

1. The first may be formulated as follows: When faced with the problem of choosing between two alternatives, one of which is an

intrinsic value and the other of which is an instrumental value, other things being equal, one ought always choose the intrinsic value. The phrase, "other things being equal," is important here especially because the conditional ought being stated is highly abstract, and because a seemingly instrumental value is not actually an instrumental value unless it actually results in an intrinsic value. Thus, if the intrinsic value involved in this instrumental value also becomes part of the perspective within which the alternatives are viewed, then the problem becomes that of choosing between one intrinsic value on the one hand and an instrumental value together with its potential intrinsic value on the other. However, many actual choices must be made between an immediately enjoyable intrinsic value and obtaining or retaining instruments whose prospects of fruitfulness remain uncertain. Here the issue of certainty versus uncertainty regarding instruments resulting in actual intrinsic values becomes paramount. For example, one may feel a need for deciding between spending his last now-available dollar for a highly praised movie, the enjoyment of which is immediate and self-terminating, as against spending it for an otherwise unobtainable highly rated book which he may never find time to read. Of course, since "other things" are seldom "equal," pride in owning such a book as well as prospective discomfort arising from needs for caring for it, storing it, dusting it, guarding it against theft, may be factors.

The foregoing discussion, focusing upon difficulties in taking the principle into consideration as such in actual decisions, should not becloud its basicness to value theory and ethics. The principle is already inherent in the distinction (and in the need for distinguishing) between intrinsic and instrumental value in the first place. Hence, insofar as one can choose between an actual intrinsic value which is an end in itself, and an instrumental value which does not have its end in itself, one ought to choose the former because intrinsic value both is the ultimate basis of choice and is intuitively apprehended as ultimate or as an end in itself whenever its nature is clearly recognized. Intrinsic value is "the end which justifies the means," and thus ought always to be preferred to the means, other things being equal.

2. The second general principle, which may seem to contradict the first, is really a necessary supplement to it. Whereas instrumental value depends upon intrinsic value teleologically (intrinsic value is the end for which instrumental value is the means), intrinsic value depends for its existence upon instrumental value causally. Hence, to the extent that an intrinsic value cannot exist without those instruments and their values as causes of it, one must treat the instruments and their values as prior to the intrinsic value to be caused. This principle may be stated as follows: When, and insofar as, instrumental value is causally prior to intrinsic value, other things being equal, one ought always choose the instrumental value or means to an end (thus obtaining both means and end) as against an end, or intrinsic value, which does not, because it cannot, exist without the means to it. These two principles do not contradict each other because the phrase, "other things being equal," contained in each of them signifies, in part, that the factors stated in the other are thereby being taken into account.

3. The third general principle incorporates the first two in a more comprehensive statement. It may be formulated as follows: When faced with the problem of choosing between two alternatives, one of which consists of both intrinsic value and instrumental value and the other of which consists of either intrinsic value or instrumental value alone, other things being equal, one ought always choose the former. Reference here is to three situations, the first of which involves both an intrinsic value enjoyed as an end in itself and an instrumental value which may lead to another intrinsic value, the second of which involves an intrinsic value enjoyed as an end in itself without an instrumental value which may lead to another intrinsic value, and the third of which involves an instrumental value which may lead to an intrinsic value without any immediately enjoyed intrinsic value as an end in itself. When faced with a problem of choosing among these three alternatives, other things being equal, one ought to choose the first because greater intrinsic value is in prospect than in the other two.

Principles for Choosing Between Intrinsic and Instrumental Values Where Production and Consumption of Instrumental Values Are At Stake

Using the terms "enjoyed" and "not enjoyed" to refer to experiences in which intrinsic values are present and absent, respectively (principles relative to intrinsic evils will be neglected here), we propose the following:

1. When faced with the problems of choosing described in the following, other things being equal, one ought to choose the first alternative : (a) Productive activity which is enjoyed and productive activity which is not enjoyed. (b) Consumptive activity which is enjoyed and consumptive activity which is not enjoyed. (c) Activity which is both productive and consumptive and enjoyed, and activity which is both productive and consumptive and not enjoyed.

2. When faced with the problem of choosing described in the following, other things being equal, one ought to choose the first alternative: (a) Productive activity which is enjoyed and consumptive activity which is enjoyed (i.e. equally). (b) Nonconsumptive activity which is enjoyed and consumptive activity which is enjoyed. (c) Activity whcih is both productive and nonconsumptive which is enjoyed and activity which is both consumptive and nonproductive which is enjoyed. One ought to choose the first in each case because, in addition to the enjoyments, presumed to be equal, instruments which may have value later are produced, not consumed, or produced and not consumed, respectively.

3. Still more complex situations exist which, because they are the same in some respects, provide a basis for formulating principles. Some of these involve "diminishing returns;" and there is a sense in which all "laws of diminishing returns" are moral laws insofar as instrumental values are involved. The first has to do with diminishing returns (i.e. actual intrinsic values enjoyed) resulting from increasing production of instruments. When a point has been reached at which additional production can result in no more enjoyment, an "ought to produce" turns into an "ought not to produce," other things being equal (i.e. do not make instruments which can never be used, when no enjoyment can come from

making them). The second has to do with diminishing returns resulting from increasing consumption of instruments. When a point has been reached at which additional consumption of instruments yields no more enjoyment, an "ought to consume" turns into an "ought not to consume," other things being equal (e.g. do not eat more candy now if taste buds are completely saturated or appetite is perfectly satiated). The third has to do with diminishing returns resulting from both increasing production and increasing consumption of instruments. When a point has been reached in the production and consumption of instruments at which additional production and consumption of instruments yields no additional enjoyment, an "ought to produce and consume" turns into an "ought not to produce and consume," other things being equal.

Principles for Choosing Between Actual and Potential Values

Since actuality of intrinsic value is the ultimate locus of power to compel our choices, any power which a supposed potential intrinsic value has for compelling our choice exists ultimately in its actuality. Hence, the obviousness of this basic principle: When faced with the problem of choosing between an actual intrinsic value and a potential intrinsic value, other things being equal, one ought to prefer the actual to the potential. However, we seldom face a problem which occurs in precisely this extremely abstract form. In fact, if the potential is a "real potential," i.e. one which will in fact result in an actual value, and not merely a "conditional potential" intrinsic value, then if the potential and the actual values are equal, other things being equal, except that time may be regarded as an insignificant factor, it may make no difference whether one enjoys the actual intrinsic value now or the actual intrinsic value which the "real potential intrinsic value" must actualize in the future. If the potential intrinsic value is merely "conditional," or if one is uncertain as to whether the potential intrinsic value is "real" or "conditional," then, other things being equal, one clearly ought to prefer the actual to the potential.

Since the applicability of the foregoing principle depends upon whether the potential intrinsic value is "real" or "conditional," perhaps a principle relative to this distinction may be found more useful. However, the high degree of uncertainty often accompanying problems concerning judgments about "conditional" and "real" potentiality tend to make issues of certainty versus uncertainty of great significance here. Since a "conditional potential intrinsic value" is one which *would* become if all other needed conditions cooperate and since a "real potential intrinsic value" is one which *will* become because all of the needed conditions will cooperate, the existence of intrinsic value is assured in the latter and not in the former case. Thus, when faced with the problem of choosing between a "conditional potential intrinsic value" and a "real potential intrinsic value," other things being equal, one ought always choose the latter.

Derivable principles relative to instrumental values are implicit in the foregoing. But we shall stop our present discussion with a summary which should prove suggestive for further independent research, though it will result in a welter of confusion if one is unable to keep constantly in mind at each step the necessary condition for adequacy of principles derivable when and insofar as "things are alike," namely, "other things being equal." When faced with the problem of ordering his preferences relative to the following items, other things being equal, one should prefer first actual intrinsic value; second, real potential intrinsic value; third, actual instrumental value (which involves real potential intrinsic value); fourth, real potential instrumental value; fifth, conditional potential intrinsic value; and finally, conditional potential instrumental value. However, since "other things" are seldom "equal," and since one may be faced with problems which are primarily causal in nature, he may find occasion for reversing his order of preferences; for to the extent that nothing can become actual which was not first potential and to the extent that a greater quantity and variety of conditional potential instruments increases the richness, etc. of potential intrinsic values, prudence may dictate concern for increasing varieties of conditionally useful instruments in the absence of more than probable assurance that some new and better actual intrinsic values will result.

Finally, we suggest that if and when one is faced with the problem of choosing between alternatives, one of which consists of both actual and potential intrinsic values and the other of either actual or potential intrinsic value alone, other things being equal, one ought always choose the former. This suggested principle should hold even if the potentiality is only "conditional" or whether one is uncertain as to whether it is "conditional" or "real."

CHAPTER 8

PERSONAL ETHICS

CONFUSION PERSISTS IN MANY QUARTERS over the issue of whether ethics properly pertains only to social affairs or also to purely individual matters. Hasty or immature conclusions about the nature of ethics, often resulting from learning about ethics in terms of negative commands by others, ignores the ultimate basis of ethics in intrinsic values experienced as feelings by individuals and in voluntary choices between alternative values experienced as feelings of oughtness. The ultimate bases of ethics are personal experiences. Not only is ethics basically individual, but many treatises on ethics limit themselves primarily to understanding such experiences. However, each person is also essentially social. He cannot be born without a mother; he cannot survive as an infant without the help of others; he cannot develop his human personality without interacting with others; many of his interests can be satisfied only, and many more can be satisfied better, through cooperation with others. Hence, even as an individual, a person depends upon others somewhat and, to the extent that he does, he automatically develops interests in others even merely as a person.

But groups also exist. Although groups depend for their existence and nature upon the persons who compose them, some groups also persist and behave as such in ways which outlast individuals, which cause persons to exist, which mold the personalities of individuals, and which control as well as serve individuals. Once a group exists, issues arise about group welfare, about conflicts between interests of the group and its members, and about conflicts between groups. Here we come to a realm which is clearly social. Ethics as a science is essentially involved

166

in both personal oughts, pertaining to each person's interests apart from others as well as his interests in others and social oughts, pertaining to each group's interests in its own welfare, including its interests in its own members and in other groups. The present chapter is devoted to the behavior of persons and the following chapter is devoted to the behavior of groups. Persons have obligations even apart from groups; but groups have no obligations apart from persons. For, as we have seen, the ultimate locus of oughtness or obligation is in the intrinsic values enjoyed or suffered by persons, and persons may enjoy or suffer alone, but groups have no experiences of enjoyment or suffering except those of persons.

Nature of Self

Disagreements among scientists about what a person ought to do often result from disagreements about the nature of self. For example, persons have been conceived as eternal souls with temporary bodies; as materialistic mechanisms; as growing biological animals; as sometimes having a static nature and sometimes a developing nature; as sometimes single and simple, sometimes dual (soul and body), sometimes multiple; as sometimes self-sufficient, sometimes wholly dependent, sometimes partly self-sufficient and partly dependent, etc. Different conceptions of the nature of a self entail differing conceptions of a self's values, of what is good for a self, and consequently of what a self ought to do to maintain or maximize those values. These disagreements are about metaphysical, biological and psychological issues primarily; and their resolution is the task of such other sciences primarily; yet ethics as a science depends for adequate solution to its own problems upon the solution of such problems by these other sciences.

We cannot explore here the many issues involved in deciding about the nature of a self. But we can propose a workable (i.e. a "working") hypothesis to serve until other sciences have done their work more conclusively. We commonly speak of a person as "having interests." One ethicist, DeWitt H. Parker, conveniently describes a person as "a bundle of interests." All such "interests" have to do, ultimately, with intrinsic and instrumental values. But we experience them in terms of needs, wants and wishes, for such things as food, shelter, clothing, health, property, friends and children. All of the different theories of self agree in this, surely, that all persons have "interests," regardless of how many, how conceived, and how described and explained. My working hypothesis proposes, as a minimum, that persons have interests, that each person has many interests, so many that they cannot all be realized, and so many that some conflict with others in such ways that one has to choose between them. A further hypothesis, stated previously, is that the need for choosing among such alternative interests is the origin of each person's oughts. The more interests one has which conflict with each other, the more often one has to choose between them and hence the more oughts which he thereby acquires.

We may, in passing, observe that although, on the one hand, we naturally tend to desire increase in abundance of opportunities so that we can have more and more alternative goods to choose from, on the other hand we also, when finding the task of choosing between alternatives more onorous, tend to desire freedom from choice. It may be that when we are more vigorous it is more fitting that we have more alternatives and while we are weaker it is more fitting that we are not required to make more choices. As ethical theory progressively adapts itself to the additional ethical problems created by living in an economy of abundance, in megalopolis, in intricately complex and swiftly changing societies, the variable problem of having too few versus too many alternatives to choose from may become a major one. As civilization complexifies itself, more intricate problems demand more sophisticated types of solutions; and, although much of the early wisdom literature of mankind contains profound insights which remain useful, newer problems, or older problems occurring with greater frequency and intensity, create conditions which make reliance upon ancient theories dangerous. Obsolescence in ethical theory is itself a major problem for ethical science, as it is for other sciences. And continued research relative to the sensitivity with which even the most advanced and seemingly most adequate theory adopted by ethical scientists continues to be adequate for changing circumstance is itself a progressively important need.

Self as Social

To the extent that a person cannot be born without a mother, cannot survive without aid from others, and cannot organize and humanize his personality without interacting with others, he depends upon others for the development of some of his interests. Sociologist Ellsworth Farris asserts that "One can no more organize his personality independently than he can be born without a mother.* Hence, one's interests in his relations with other people are an essential part of the interests of every person who thus depends upon others for his welfare and happiness. Social psychologist, W. I. Thomas, has proposed as a working hypothesis the view that all human interests can be grouped, for convenience, into four kinds which may be called "the wish for security," with its negative counterpart, the wish for freedom from fear; "the wish for recognition" or esteem, and for freedom from humiliation; "the wish for response," companionship or love, and for freedom from loneliness; and "the wish for new experience," curiosity, adventure or freedom from boredom.* Although persons differ regarding how they conceive security, esteem, love and adventure, all have some interests in each of these areas. The point I wish to emphasize here is that, in all of these areas, most persons tend to find that some of their interests can be satisfied better through social cooperation.

British philosopher Herbert Spencer has shown how, by cooperative efforts, weaker persons have been able to overcome stronger enemies, division of labor has enabled people to survive and prosper, and specialization has resulted in common benefits not otherwise possible. Also, differing moral systems, especially those in which selfishness is discouraged and in-group altruism is encouraged, have proved advantageous in the struggle for existence and survival of the fit. Once issues of selfishness versus consideration for others arise, as they do for every infant not too long after birth, then the question faces every self as to what policy is best in pursuing its own interests in each social relation.

---

*Ellsworth Farris, *The Nature of Human Nature* (New York, McGraw-Hill, 1937), p. 279.
*William I. Thomas and Florian Znaniecki, *The Polish Peasant in Europe and America* (New York, Knopf, 1918, 1927), vol. I, p. 73.

To the extent that each self depends upon others for his welfare, and for the satisfaction of his wishes (in each of Thomas' four groups, for example), he needs to know how to act in order to best accomplish his ends. Such issues are of so great importance that some people believe that problems are not properly called ethical until conflict of interests of different persons arise. They are of such significance that our earliest wisdom literature deals directly with them. And some of the earliest insights pertaining to simple human relationships may never be improved upon.

Early and late, men discover a natural principle of reciprocity, in both physics and ethics, which appears to operate with varying degrees of reliability, depending upon differing circumstances in which "other things are not equal." Just as in physics the hypothesis that for every action there is an equal and opposite reaction has been found very useful in understanding and in improving our adaptations to and our control over physical processes, so in ethics the hypothesis that each person tends to treat others as he believes he is being treated by them also has been found useful in understanding human relations and in increasing the satisfactions which may be obtained through cooperative action in accordance with it. Hindus early formulated it as a "law of Karma." Primitive peoples, whether or not they personified the powers in nature upon which they believed their welfare depended, developed beliefs about justice such that individuals and groups need to make gifts, either to initiate or to repay, for benefits expected or received. Although properly called "sacrifices," i.e. making "holy" or whole, restitution of justice in accordance with an underlying principle of reciprocity appears to have been implicit. Confucius, who claimed to have derived his views from the wisdom of the ancients prior to his time, employed this principle in formulating his rule for the best way of doing things in social relationships: Do not do unto others what you do not want others to do to you. Later Jesus formulated "the Golden rule," do unto others as you would have others do unto you." These simple statements receive more profound interpretations as, for example, when Confucius discriminates differences in equality which must be taken into account also; for a father should treat his son as he would like to be treated if he were his son, rather than as an exact equal when

he is not.* Jesus preferred love to rigid justice, or rather advocated that it is best to love others enough to be willing to forgive
them, not merely "as we are forgiven," but also "seventy times
seven." Why? Because we too, reciprocally, need to be loved and
forgiven in the same spirit.

A person's interests in others is of two sorts, as means and as
ends. That is, a person who has interests which can be satisfied
only by means of others thereby is interested in using others as
means to his ends. But also, since, despite the privacy of our own
enjoyments, we also develop humanity only as we also develop
sympathetic insight into, and sympathy both for and with, the
enjoyments and sufferings of others, we can enjoy "sharing our
feelings" with others to the extent that our own feelings are
thereby enhanced. One person does not love another deeply until
he enjoys his own appreciation of the other as an end in himself.
And, reciprocally, one cannot expect to be appreciated as an end
in himself unless he does the same for others. A person who does
not love cannot expect to be loved. To the extent that a desire to
be loved is normal to human nature, here is one interest which
depends for its realization upon acting upon the principle of
reciprocity.

The following ten principles which constitute an additional
hypothesis can be experimented with both by each individual and
by public, intercultural, worldwide research projects. Let us summarize my illustration relative to Thomas' "wish for recognition"
or esteem.*

1. Recognition is necessarily social; for to be esteemed one must
be esteemed by others.

2. To be esteemed, one must somehow do or be what others
admire.

3. One naturally likes to be admired. So, when admired, he
seeks to continue and increase such admiration.

4. Desire for more approval tends to shade imperceptibly into
desire for more approval that one will receive.

5. Desire for more approval than one will receive begets unfortunate consequences. For one's belief that he deserves more

---

*Archie J. Bahm, *The Heart of Confucius* (New York, Walker, 1969).
*Developed more fully in *Why Be Moral?*, Ch. 5.

than he receives implies distrust of the opinions of others. Others, finding themselves distrusted, hence disapproved, tend to reciprocate by disapproving such distrust. Hence, excessive desire for recognition is self-defeating.

6. A principle of reciprocity seems inherent in human nature, which works both negatively and positively. Slap me and I will want to slap you. Condemn me and I will want to condemn you, at least for condemning me. Admire me, and I will admire you, at least for admiring me.

7. One may help satisfy his desire for esteem (a) by not despising others and (b) by appreciating others. That is, he may deliberately withhold disesteem and initiate esteem of others. Self-interestedness, or desiring what is best for oneself, should not be mistaken for selfishness, which consists in intending to obtain more than one deserves at the expense of others. The more you desire to increase your esteem, the more unselfish you should be in esteeming others.

8. The principle of reciprocity usually reflects sincerity and insincerity. If one evaluates others insincerely, his insincerity tends to be reciprocated.

9. The principle does not work with mathematical precision. Delay should be expected in receiving some rewards. When coming later, they often appear as surprises. If your gift was genuine, you expect no return; so when returns arrive unexpectedly, they may appear as more than deserved. Of course, others may forget our appreciation of them even as we forget their appreciation of us. But people who practice the principle testify that they come out ahead in the long run.

10. To the extent that the principle does work, each person has within his own power a means for increasing the satisfaction of his interest in recognition.

Conflicts of Interests

Conflicts of interests are normal. Conflicts of many kinds are normal. Postponing consideration of conflicts pertaining to group interests until the following chapter, we concentrate here upon those inherent in personal ethics. In addition to (a) those conflicts which are of a purely private nature, such as choosing between interesting books while reading oneself to sleep at night, we all encounter at least the following kinds. (b) In his relations with another person in whom he is interested, a person often needs to choose between pursuing his interests in that person versus purely private interests. For example, he may have to decide whether to loan a book or to read it himself. (c) He may have to choose between which of two things he can do for another person. If the other is a guest, he may have to decide whether to take him out to eat or to serve him at home. (d) When regarding another as an end in himself with his own private interests, one may have to choose between his interest in having his friend be useful to him and permitting him to pursue his own private or other social interests. For example, if one author has invited another as an overnight guest, and they have finished their planned consultations, then should the host urge his guest to spend remaining time criticizing his manuscript or urge the guest to then work upon the guest's own manuscript? (e) When a person is interested in two persons more or less equally, such as two parents, two children, two siblings or two pupils, he often finds that there are times when he must choose between favoring one or the other with his attention, assistance, affection. If a man has two intimate girlfriends, both of whom he would like to marry, then the greater his interest in both, the greater his conflict of interests when the time comes for a final decision. (f) Such conflicts of interests appearing relative to two persons tend to multiply as one develops interests in three, four or many persons, equally or unequally. The more friends one has, the more intimate relatives one has, and the more acquaintances one has acquired, the greater the number of conflicts of interests which result from having limited amounts of time, energy or money with which to pursue all such interests.

The foregoing samples of conflicts of interests exemplify typical kinds of situations in which obligations arise. The point being emphasized here is that, even merely as personal, i.e. so far as the interests of a person are concerned, many of his oughts involve others because he has interests in those others. And awareness of the principle of reciprocity emerges in his own experience, partly because he has interests in others and partly because people tend to treat each other as they are treated by others. Before passing on to social ethics, i.e. the ethics of group behavior, we may wish to be reminded that ethics as a science may be required to establish at least some of its needed conclusions relative to personal ethics before it can hope for much success in demonstrating its generalizations relative to the much more complicated situations occurring in social ethics.

CHAPTER 9

SOCIAL ETHICS

SOCIAL ETHICS PERTAINS TO GROUPS. Hence, a primary requisite for an adequate social ethics is an adequate social science, i.e. sociology together with those sciences which deal with specialized aspects of group behavior, such as economics, political science, social psychology and anthropology. Some of the confusion attributed to ethical theory and practice results from disagreements remaining among social scientists. Of course, the reverse is also true. That is, social ethics as a science is a social science, and inadequacy in its development makes its own contribution to deficiencies in other social sciences all of which interdepend in various ways.

The Nature of Groups

In general, a group consists of two or more persons consciously associating or interacting, directly or indirectly. Some groups are merely temporary, even momentary and casual. But we shall direct our attention to more permanent groupings. Following sociologist Cooley, we find the distinction between "primary" and "nonprimary" groups very enlightening.

Family groups, children's play groups and primitive village neighborhoods, which consist of relatively intimate, face-to-face, unspecialized associations, are called primary because "they are fundamental in forming the social nature and ideals of the individual" and they "are springs of life, not only for the individual, but for social institutions.* Without primary association, wherein ideals of individual worth and group loyalty develop, human

---

*Charles Horton Cooley et al., *Introductory Sociology* (New York, Charles Scribner's Sons, 1933), pp. 55, 59.

nature would not emerge in the biological baby nor could other more complex and specialized groups arise with stabilized sentiments and habitualized attitudes of agreement in the individuals who form their bases. "This humanizing of animal drives is perhaps the greatest service performed by the primary group,"[†] partly because it gives the child something which it does not have at birth and which makes both his remaining life and nature possible, and partly because the whole existence of society depends squarely upon the standards of value he develops there.

Nonprimary groups—those where association is more specialized, partial and impersonal—are possible only because the ideals developed in primary groups gradually become extended as the person grows in awareness of the values of larger and more specialized groups to his own welfare. Both in the history of the race and in the life of each person, there develop wider ranges of "we-feelings." Each infant grows through expanding his feelings of identity with parents, playmates, neighborhood, school groups, community, state, nation and mankind. He who cannot grow up to cooperate within the limits of local consensus is imprisoned, asylumed, exiled or killed. Nonprimary or "secondary" association has some tremendous advantages which "may be summed up as those resulting mainly from specialization, impersonality, reach and continuity."[‡] Specialization and division of labor result in richer varieties and greater quantities of complicated and skillfully produced goods and services; e.g. not merely economic (farm, factory, mine, store, bank) but also educational, religious, political, medical, recreational and the many specialized subdivisions of these. Impersonality simplifies social adjustment problems by standardizing our contacts so that interactions between people become habitual and automatic rather than recurringly problematic, difficult and uncertain. "Reach" means that we can share the fruits of distant peoples and feel at home in a larger world. "Continuity" refers to the perpetuation of institutionalized values and functions from generation to generation, so that persons born today enjoy a much richer heritage than primitive peoples.

---

†*Ibid.*, p. 59.
‡*Ibid.*, p. 215.

But "secondary association is partial association. It is association narrowed down by special purpose, by communications at a distance, by rules, by social barriers, or by the casual nature of contact. This means that under such conditions associating personalities present only special facets of themselves to one another. They cannot meet as whole persons."* Such association suffers from certain dangers which "lie chiefly in the social illiteracy of the narrow specialist, in the functionary's tendency to disregard human values, in the inertia of great organizations, and in the resulting readjustment lag." Increasing stress upon specialization magnifies specialization in partiality rather than in wholeness. The more fully a person devotes himself to his specialty, the more he cuts off parts of his personality from association with others. Even in the same university, different specialists often cannot understand each other's language. Furthermore, "it is a fatally short step from the impersonal to the inhuman. . . . Large organizations have an inertia much greater than primary groups. . . . The lag between need and readjustment tends to be longer."† Thus, although expansion of personality profits greatly by extension and growth in efficiency of secondary groups, the benefits are bought at a price. A person's confidence that he is valued as an end in himself tends to decline as increase in nonprimary association decreases the proportion of time spent in intimate, face-to-face, whole-personality association. Consequently his sense of loyalty, fair play, devotion to others tends to decline and the wholesome feelings that come from belonging tend to be replaced gradually by disregard not only for local mores but even for all morality in general. Human nature becomes dehumanized.

Nonprimary groups are of two major types, those geographically oriented and those growing up around specialized functions and purposes. Geographically organized groups include the local community, the county, the municipality, the state, the region, the nation, continental organizations of nations and all of humanity. (Interplanetary societies remain in the planning stage at this writing.) Such groups tend to be multipurpose groups and are

---

Ibid., p. 214.
†*Ibid.*, pp. 217-218.

concerned with the general welfare of the area. Most of them contain subdivisions and participate as parts in larger area orga- nizations, and most of them have specialized agencies (legislative, administrative, judicial) and policies regarding kinds of functions performed by the public group and private agencies. Special pur- pose groups, which may serve only one purpose exclusively or may be organized to serve several purposes, are exemplified by school districts (including subgroups such as first grade teachers), retail distribution stores (including subgroups such as hardware stores, with subgroups such as departments specializing in metal windows and fixtures), manufacturing groups (including cement block manufacturing, which includes pumice block makers) and transportation systems (including automobile traffic regulation, including departments making traffic signs).

Ethical problems and principles relevant thereto differ in de- tails relative to each kind of purpose and function, and differ greatly in highly specialized groups as compared to geographically organized general or multipurpose groups, since the latter have comprehensive responsibilities and obligations with which they are directly concerned, whereas special purpose groups tend to have them much less directly though they do have them to the extent that they cannot carry out their own functions unless mini- mal conditions of security prevail in the general purpose group. But in addition to differing ethical problems there are also ethical problems common to all of them. For example, the following typical kinds of relationships exist in all or most of them; conflicts of interests may, and typically do, exist relative to each of these kinds.

1. Each group has relation to its members. Most groups have requirements, whether explicitly stated or merely understood, about who can be a member, about duties of members to the group and duties of the group to members, or about rights of members and rights of the group, about group justice to members, both retribu- tive (e.g. taxes to members or benefits to members) and distribu- tive (i.e. equal treatment between equal members and equally unequal treatment of unequal members, as when a group taxes a wage earner but not an infant), and conditions for terminating membership.

2. Each group has some self-interest as a group. A group has a duty to perpetuate itself so long as its functions are needed by members; if the group's purpose is merely temporary, such as a party to celebrate the end of a school year, then it has a duty to terminate itself rather than to perpetuate itself (i.e. have all its bills paid before ceasing to exist). Geographically organized groups need to protect their territory; to determine their boundaries; to see that all of the different kinds of specialized functions are cared for; to maintain internal security and health; to minimize internal conflicts of interests; to elect or appoint officers to perform needed functions; to determine how many functions shall be publicly and how many privately allocated; to treat its officers fairly, including having policies regarding tenure in office, pay, penalties for failure in duties, conditions and methods for removal, and methods of receiving new members. Each special purpose group may have similar functions, or interests, and ethical problems, except that they tend to have limited powers and responsibilities, as indicated by "Ltd.," required after some corporation names. Large groups always require some method for delegating responsibilities and duties, together with rules.

3. Each group (except humanity or a universally effective world government) has peer groups. So relationships, interests and ethical problems typical to peer groups may be studied as such. For example, two counties in a state, two states in a nation, two nations in a world organization have problems involved in relating to each other as groups of their own kind, together with many subproblems, such as exchange of citizens, trade, a subgroup in one country operating as a subgroup in another country (e.g. an oil company in one country obtaining drilling, extracting and exporting rights in another country), border disputes, criminal escapees and differential currency exchanges and balance of payments problems. Examples of special purpose peer groups are two competing gas stations, a drug versus a grocery store, two insurance companies or two air transport companies. Ethical problems of "fair" competition, cooperation and combination tend to have some common characteristics, and many of these have been studied scientifically and some have been legislated about extensively.

4. Except for those groups on the bottom of the social hierarchy, each group has subgroups.

5. Except for that group which is at the top of the, or a, social hierarchy, each group is a part of, even a member of, a larger group. Typical as well as unique problems occur in the relationships between higher- and lower-level groups. Although they are not exactly analogous to those relationships of a group to its members who are persons, since persons are themselves the locus of intrinsic value, many of them are similar because they do function as instrumental values which do have responsibilities ultimately to persons. Just as some groups have persons as members with limited rights and duties, so some groups have other groups as members with limited rights and duties. Included among the problems are those of the relation of officers, for example, of a group several levels up the hierarchy to officers of groups several levels lower.

6. This brings us to the problem of conflicts of interests between all of the preceding kinds of groups and group interests. The point being stressed here again is that ethics as a field is of such immense complexity that many give up trying to understand it while others remain confused because they try to use principles which are suited in one type of social relationship that turns out to be unsuited to different types. The urgent need for a well-developed science of ethics should become more obvious as one becomes better acquainted with the complexities all of which require specialized investigation.

The Nature Culture: Mores, Institutions, Laws

Just as each individual person profits by developing habits, so that having gone to the trouble of figuring out the best adjustment pattern in dealing with a particular kind of problem will not have to be repeated, so persons in groups profit by developing common behavior patterns relative to certain kinds of adjustment problems and of adopting them as habits. One problem involved in inducting infants into adult societies is that they do not always foresee or understand importance of the problems to which the mores and institutions are adaptations. And, since individual and group interests are often at variance, groups find it necessary to urge, and even enforce, conformity on the part of individual members whenever the individual's behavior is likely to put the group, or the individual himself, in jeopardy.

Sociologists distinguish between folkways, mores and laws. All these may be said to be "institutions" in the sense that they become established, stable or permanent structurings of behavior. Folkways are commonly participated-in behavior patterns which are not enforced. For example, my coat has a notch in its lapel and buttons on its sleeves because everybody wears coats that way; but if I chose to have a coat without notch or buttons, no one would regard my behavior as immoral. But mores are those common behavior patterns which a group does regard as somehow important to group welfare and so conformity is expected and persons who do not conform are regarded as immoral. Now mores differ in importance and so the importance of conformity varies. Those which are regarded with great importance often have penalties attached to nonconformity. With the advent of explicit legislation, whether by a ruler, a law-giver or an established legislative body, then explicit penalties can be attached, and the severity of the penalty should properly be evaluated realtive to the greatness of the danger to group welfare.

Once penalties are assessed, then problems of enforcement arise, both regarding apprehension of nonconformists, judging their "guilt," evaluating and assessing the penalty, and collecting the penalty. Ordinary mores tend to be opinion-enforced; if one does not conform, others will disapprove his behavior, maybe scorn him, perhaps refuse to cooperate with him. But laws normally have, in addition, official enforcement and hence officers charged with duties and responsibilities to enforce them. Police, courts, juries, jails and prisons all result from these typical social needs. However, difficulties occur, not merely because particular individuals do not understand the mores or laws or because conflicts of interests are such that individuals choose to violate mores or laws, but also because the laws themselves are regarded unjust or evil. We mention only two sources of such injustice.

1. A ruler may have been angry or ignorant in proclaiming the law, or the legislature may have been maliciousy influenced or ignorant in legislating. Systems of legislation themselves may be

better or worse, and when special interests are favored by legislation, then enforcement of unfair laws causes citizens to distrust the law. Such distrust, unfortunately, may then spread to additional laws, and group welfare is endangered when group loyalty declines.

2. Cultural lag occurs when mores or laws, no matter how well adapted to the adjustment problems to which they were solutions, continue to exist and to be enforced after the need for conformity has declined or ceased to exist. Of course, there can be lag also in failure to adopt laws needed for new problems (e.g. village waited until deaths resulted from twenty traffic accidents before installing stop signals), and in failing to adopt needed new laws after old ones are repealed. As changes—whether technological, industrial, populational or educational — occur with increasing rapidity, need for more rapid adoption of new and repeal of old laws arises. But changing mores and some laws (e.g. constitutions), like persons changing habits, is not something that can be done easily. Nothing is closer to the heart of ethical theory and practice than issues involved in cultural lag and the ways and means and needs for overcoming such lag.

I find C.H. Cooley's theory of "The Cycle of Institutional Development"* a most helpful generalization for understanding the problems, processes and ethical implications typical of cultural lag situations. After (1) "incipient organization," when the institution is being conceived, examined, experimented with and adopted, there tends to develop (2) a stage of "efficiency," wherein members believe that the mores or laws serve their needs and when they tend to participate or conform willingly. But as times change, new problems arise and old ones disappear or become relatively insignificant, or when the cost of conformity is greater than the benefits received from conformity, then continuing conformity represents (3) a state of "formalism." "Formalism" is a stage where people feel compelled to conform, and officials to enforce conformity, even though the values originally resulting from conformity no longer exist and when the purposes which the institution was designed to serve are no longer relevant. At this

---

*Ibid., pp. 406-415.

stage, enforcement is often literal rather than vital, for the enforcing officer knows what the law says even though he now may not know its purpose. When the purpose of the law is clear from awareness of the benefits being derived, then both officer and violator can understand the reason for conformity, for enforcement and for occasions for pliability in conformity and enforcement in order to serve the purposes better. But when the purpose and values are forgotten, only the letter of the law remains. Intolerance often accompanies such sterility. And respect for law declines.

"Disorganization" results when increasing numbers refuse to conform. Not only do people and officials loose interest in, and become antagonistic to, institutions which require services but give no benefits no matter how habitual, but also new members of the group cannot willingly be induced to accept institutions which have ceased to be useful. During this stage, those who conform regard nonconformists as immoral, while those who do not conform regard those who do as stupid or old-fashioned. Increase in delinquency and crime, as measured by the previously existing standards, increases. And, unfortunately, when disrespect for one law carries over into disrespect for other laws, including those which are useful, disorganization tends to disrupt the society as a whole and the value of the group itself may be seriously threatened. If the original need giving rise to an institution has disappeared, sooner or later it disintegrates. But if the orginal need exists, but in a modified form, or if new needs exist which partially incorporate the original need, reorganization occurs typically. New institutions or modifications of old institutions arise; and they too may then pass through the stages of efficiency, formalism and disorganization.

Without taking time to explore various additional complexities involved in Cooley's theory, we can note some ethical implications. To the extent that institutions—whether mores, laws, corporate structures or other aspects of culture such as language habits—have instrumental value for members, the greater their instrumental value the more such values should be exploited by groups. Since the stage of efficiency is that in which the greatest benefits appear to be derived from participation, members and officers of groups ought to try to maintain institutions longest in this stage. Since the stages of formalism and disorganization result in more evil than good, these periods, together with those of dis-integration of evil and reorganization of good institutions, should be hastened as much as possible. John Dewey has advocated increase in "social intelligence" by which he means the ability of societies to escape cultural lag as much as possible, by deliberately attending to the status of institutions and of replacing old with new as rapidly as cultural lag occurs. Some legislatures have re-search divisions which advise repeal of obsolete laws and antici-pate needs for future laws. Corporations often devote considerable investment in planning for the future.

As societies become more complex and interdependent, the im-portance of needed flexibility as well as of needed stability and of social intelligence becomes greater. As societies become more complex, more complex forms of stability are needed; since stable elements in each of the areas tend to give additional support to the stability in every other area, the overall rigidity of the system increases. As counter-need for greater flexibility also increases, the problems involved in overcoming cultural lag increase, and the ways and means may become different in kind and quality as a result. Ethical aspects of the issues involved may be observed by examining the differences between evolutionary versus revolution-ary methods of reform or reorganization.

Although, on the one hand, the differences between evolution and revolution may be regarded as differences in degree rather than in kind, when differences in degree become sufficiently great they tend to become differences in kind. Culture, although by its very nature as something which is learned by being handed down from genera-tion to generation, so to speak, is something stable. Yet, also, cul-ture changes in the sense that new ideas or behavior traits are added, some are discontinued and some are modified. When cultural change is relatively slow and gradual, we tend to speak of it as evolutionary; when it becomes relatively more rapid or complete, we tend to call it revolutionary. One difficulty with his distinction is that a change within one cultural area, such as a business practice or a marriage law, may be great, hence revolutionary; whereas, in relation to the culture as a whole, it is relatively minor, hence evolutionary. Furthermore, the word "revolution" applies also to political changes, as when elected officials of the party in office are defeated and replaced by officials of an opposing party without any significant cultural changes. The goods and evils of political revolutions are themselves matters of ethical evaluation, but our concern here is primarily with culture.

Ours is a time of revolutionary cultural changes, i.e. greater than usual changes have been occurring in many or most areas of life. Furthermore, changes in one area increasingly interdepend with those in other areas. Likewise, the kinds and quantity of changes are such that they are increasing in profundity, extending to the philosophical foundations of our cultural system. When all of the intellectual and value foundations of a society become questioned, disorganization affects the whole society. Some see ours as a time characterized by an increasing moral vacuum. Old explanations and old ideals of what is good or best in life have been challenged without there appearing among the new candidates already being experimented with a new world view, *weltanschauung*, i.e. explanation and set of ideals which can command universal appeal. The problem of reconstructing our world view may be our most important ethical problem, if not today because we are not yet ready, then early tomorrow. That is, what ought our world view to be is itself a question to which a fully adequate ethical science should address itself.*

When cultural revolution becomes more drastic, the personality crises of more persons whose habits of believing and acting regarding value ideals are more severe, because what one has believed to be true and good is now claimed to be false and evil. When a person who, having sought the truest and best, has lived his life more or less successfully according to his long-accepted beliefs is challenged to admit that these beliefs are now false, he responds with reluctance to say the least. Persons whose habit patterns are more firmly established often reject the challenge itself as false and evil, whereas those who have developed habits of flexibility may accept

---

*For suggestions which include some principles for choosing among world views, see *Why Be Moral?*, Ch. 34.

the newer ideals and practices with ease. But since achievement of considerable stability, hence rigidity, in all who have achieved moral and philosophical habits is to be expected as normal, the more revolutionary the changes the more traumatic does enforcement of changes in such habits tend to be. When cultural lag accumulates too long and the habits of those in charge maintaining "the establishment" are too rigid to change evolutionarily, then political revolution becomes more likely. The terrific costs of political revolutions in which the personal welfare of whole populations are at stake stagger the imagination. In a contrast to a mere *coup d'état,* where one power group replaces another without affecting the culture, a political revolution in which the moral and philosophical ideals of multitudes of people are jeopardized tends to be catastrophic.†

Failure to develop ethics as a science, in an age idealizing science, is itself a significant factor among those causing our current revolutions. For the refusal of those who idealize science, and who thereby in effect proclaim an ethic relative to such ideals, to apply their ideals to the field of ethics itself amounts, in the eyes of critics, to be a fundamental form of hypocrisy. Cultural revolution, in which one set of ideals has served as a rationale, and thus as a basis for rationality, is being replaced by another set of ideals which is claimed to be better and therefore more reasonable, the clash of rationalities is characterized by much irrationality. When persons on each side see themselves as having superior reasons and those on the other side as irrational, they often regard the use of irrational methods in fighting for their side justified by the seeming irrationality of the other side. Hence, from a perspective in which evolutionary changes are better because less costly than revolutionary changes, the seeming justification of increasingly irrational actions of both rebels and reactionaries promotes both cultural and personal insanity.

This book is being written, belatedly and perhaps too late, partly in the hope that those who idealize science can undergo a sufficient-

---

†For a good summary hypothesis about the natural history of a revolution, see Mabel A. Elliot and Francis E. Merrill, Revolution. In *Social Disorganization* (New York, Harper and Brothers, 1934), Ch. 31.

ly rapid revolution relative to ethics so that research and reformulation of workable ethical ideals can produce a rationale more acceptable to all, i.e. both sides of our cultural conflicts, than ideals likely to arise out of the chaos of catastrophic revolution. Doubtless, at this writing, even a crash research program will be too late; but since science itself, as a method and as a source of and sustainer of our so-called "industrial-military complex," is under attack by many cultural revolutionaries, critical self-examination in the face of such charges of hypocrisy seems called for.

Policy Decisions

Corporation management, public and private, is constantly involved in making decisions, both about particular transactions and about policies. As society and its corporations become more complicated, management responsibilities become divided and distributed at various levels. Top-level managers tend to be more preoccupied with policy decisions. And the need for training more and more persons capable of handling policy decision problems is one of the greatest. All policy decision problems are essentially ethical problems. The task is to take into consideration all of the relevant factors, i.e. conditional oughts, and to reach the best conclusion, i.e. the conclusion as to how actions by corporation personnel in accordance with policies adopted will bring about the best results for the corporation (including all those persons, etc., dependent upon it).

Perhaps because of the unpopularity of the word "ethics," and to misunderstandings, confusions and disagreements commonly associated with the term, the language "science of policy decision making" has come to replace it. Apparently and unfortunately this has grown as an extremely specialized science, and one which remains in its infancy. The magnitude of the need for competence in managerial decisions has forced development of rule-of-thumb policies about policy making, or working hypotheses derived from observing the practical consequences of successful and unsuccessful efforts at policy decision making. Since such methods are the best if not the only one available, we should all be thankful with efforts to improve the competence of those dealing with ethically important decisions. But surely we will all be better off when the relatively successful methods adopted by several corporations have been scientifically studied and generalized upon and interrelated with scientifically reached conclusions about the fundamentals of ethical theory generally.

If universities, foundations and public education supporters cannot be roused to fund research into ethics as a science, then doubtless the continuing need by private corporations for more reliable policy-decision theory may induce them to finance research into ethics as a science. It would be unfortunate if achievements to be expected from such research become the private property of certain corporations who may then use their superior knowledge to competitive advantage. For our whole civilization, sinking ever more rapidly into a moral chaos, is in great need. Even alert private corporations should now be aware of the practical value to their own selfish interests to have a society in which certain minimums of ethical agreement and moral stability prevail so that they can continue in business.

Part of the tragedy of our time is the failure of professional philosophers, i.e. those who are professional ethicists, to develop ethics as a science. Professional philosophers, unfortunately, have been among those most guilty of neglect, since direct attack upon problems in ethical theory is primarily their responsibility. A specialized philosophical society has been developed for every specialized area in the field of philosophy (e.g. logic, aesthetics, metaphysics) except one, namely, ethics. Only a handful of philosophers, outside the Roman Catholic and Pragmatic traditions, have been willing to use the word "science" in connection with ethics. This time philosophers have been followers, not leaders, in developing ideals beneficial to society. And the growth of both sophistry and anti-rational tendencies is partly a response to popular apathy and prejudice against developing ethics as a science, and partly, in turn, a cause for increasing such apathy and entrenchment of such prejudice. The evidence that "philosophy is dead" continues to mount.

But the fundamental need for fundamentally sound philosophical insights is so great that the continuing demands for them are a part of the motivation for current cultural revolution. One of the rebel cries which we have yet to hear, at least in this form, is one which will appear when the destructive anarchists give way to constructive visionaries who have achieved new philosophical ideals. With apologies to someone, "Philosophy is dead! Long live philosophy!" or "Ethics is dead! Long live ethics!"

Attention should be called to another related development resulting from growth in computer technology. Programmers limited to an ultra-simple two-valued logic face the challenge of developing techniques for reproducing models of intricately complex systems. Now systems have organization, structure, unity as well as multiplicity. Each type of problem programmed, whether payroll accounting, missile trajectory, stock market variation probabilities or public opinion trends, involves discovery or invention of some workable system. Enough of these have already been worked out so that we now have persons interested in generalizing about such systems who have developed a new science, called "general systems theory," and a thirteen-year-old Society for General Systems Research which publishes an annual, *General Systems*. The generalizing involved is a philosophical enterprise. Since the concerns of computer owners, computer technicians, programmers and systems theorists are practical, the problems with which they deal are basically value problems. They are interested in better methods of getting more and better results. Their interests and efforts are thus essentially ethical in nature. Thus the generalizations of both particular technicians and general systems theorists involve both knowledge of processes and ideals of values. Hence both are involved in new kinds of ethical problems and the need for new scientific studies relative to those problems.

One interesting aspect of this development is that the understanding of physical systems, for example, involves also idea systems or belief systems. So general systems theory has been forced to become interested in belief systems and in generalizations about them. Curiously enough, generalizations about such belief systems, when the beliefs include fundamental or foundational beliefs, are properly called "philosophy." But when the history of philosophy has been preoccupied with seemingly abstruse issues; and the study

of it tends to perpetuate old controversies; and increasing satura-
tion of philosophy departments by sophists which has provided
evidence that "philosophy is dead"; and existentialistic voluntarists
have eulogized absurdity, nothingness or death as irrational motives
for still willing to live, then general systems theorists wisely ignore
the term. One effect of this trend is that the term "belief system"
has become a substitute for a "philosophy," and general systems
theorists have become our newest, even if highly specialized, philosophers. And many professional philosophers are not even aware
that they have been effectively replaced.

Unfortunately, the kind of philosophy being developed by general
systems theorists is conditioned by limitations of computers, ma-
chinery, a two-valued symbolic logic, apparent contradictions
involved in deriving the unity required for a system from the postu-
lated completely external relation between the two values basic to
the logic, and by the inexperience of programmers and systems
theorists in dealing with the typical subtleties recurrent in philosophical problems. Just as the "ethics" described by other specialized
scientist—such as anthropologists, sociologists, economists, political
scientists, theologians, metaphysicians, linguistic philosophers and
business administrators—is depicted as a dependent aspect of their
own science and conceived in terms of its services to their science,
thereby distorting and often misconceiving its basic nature, so the
workable conclusions reached by general systems theorists about
ethics and philosophy generally is almost bound to be deficient and
slanted in ways found necessary by the conditions which give rise
to it. The cure for this deficiency, and at the same time the deficiencies of the slanted views developed by other specialized sciences
about ethics, is to attack the basic nature and problems of ethics
directly by means of scientific methods. If older philosophers are
incapable of doing this, then we must await the emergence of new
ones not crippled by established biases. But such training takes
time. And the needs for reliable results from ethics as a science
appear to be accumulating like a crescendo.

The magnitude and complexity of problems in ethics, in addition
to the simpler and more foundational problems we have mentioned,
make even the problem of outlining the kinds of research projects

needed and of ordering them in some range of priority is itself something to grapple with. Probably work should go forth at both the levels of individual and social ethics at the same time, with efforts to interrelate, both critically and integratively, projects and results at both, or various, levels.

For the present, I can only offer some initial suggestions regarding hypotheses about some principles for choosing for a group, to which the next chapter is devoted.

CHAPTER 10

PRINCIPLES FOR CHOOSING
FOR A GROUP

S OCIAL ETHICS, AS A STUDY of ethical problems and principles
pertaining to groups, involves consideration of a group's
obligations (1) to its members, both (a) as persons (who exist as
much more than as members of each group) and (b) as members
(i.e. as persons constituting the particular group); (2) to itself as
a group, both (a) as a behavioral entity having interests in its own
survival and welfare as distinct from its interests in its members
and in other groups, and (b) as a behavioral entity organically
embodying both its interests in its own survival and welfare and its
interests in its members and other groups; and (3) to other groups,
including peer groups, subordinate groups and superordinate
group, if any. We cannot here explore all these kinds of obligations.
In what follows, we excerpt from Chapter 23 of *Why Be Moral?*
most of the principles developed there pertaining to choosing for
a group in sense (2) (b) above.

We are not concerned here with the problem of who does the
choosing, but with kinds of principles which anyone faced with
the problem of choosing may call upon as aids when relevant.
Responsible officers, interested group members, and theorists and
other observers may all employ them when relevant. Although they
appear to me to be intuitively obvious, they are proposed here as
hypotheses for testing, and they can be tested by numerous relatively
direct and indirect methods.

The statement of these principles presuppose the statements
previously made in Chapter 7. Those should be reviewed before
reading further here. We cannot stress too often that each principle

192

is stated as something universal only if, or to the extent that, "all other things are equal," which, of course, they seldon, if ever, are. This precaution is one essential to the nature of scientific method, not something peculiar to ethics as a science.

Three kinds of principles are proposed, namely those pertaining to both intrinsic and instrumental values, those pertaining primarily to intrinsic values, and those pertaining primarily to instrumental values.

Principles Pertaining to Both Intrinsic and Instrumental Values

We select only one: Always choose the greatest good for the group. This is a most general, and most obvious, principle relative to choosing for any group when all other things are equal. It involves, more specifically, choosing good in preference to evil, the better of two or more goods, the lesser of two or more evils, and the better in preference to the worse.

Principles Pertaining Primarily to Intrinsic Values

These presuppose understanding of the nature of intrinsic values and the nature of persons as having or being intrinsic values and that they have intrinsic value even as members of a group. Although the theory of values sketched in Part I has been presupposed in formulating them, I believe that they will be found to hold also for at least some other theories of the nature of intrinsic values and of persons as ends in themselves. We divide these principles into two groups, (1) those pertaining to circumstances where the group is regarded as a fixed entity so far as its number of members is concerned, and (2) those pertaining to circumstances where the group is considered as variable so far as the number of its members is concerned.

Group Number Fixed

Again the problems and principles differ depending upon whether the intrinsic value per member is considered (a) invariable (fixed, incomparable) or (b) variable.

INTRINSIC VALUE PER MEMBER INVARIABLE. The term "invariable" here refers to situations in which the intrinsic value of a person is regarded as remaining unchanged, equal or alike, to the extent that the principle applies. No problems occur for decision and no principles for choosing exist when no change in the number of group members having unchanging intrinsic value is possible, other things being equal. Problems and principles pertaining to efforts needed to maintain the status quo may exist, but these have to do with instrumental values, and will be dealt with later. We can say of such a group that it is good; and we can compare it with other groups which have more or fewer members and can say that it contains less or more intrinsic value; but so long as there is nothing that can be done about improving or preventing the degeneration of such intrinsic good, no moral problem can exist relating to it and no principles for choosing are relevant.

INTRINSIC VALUE PER MEMBER VARIABLE. If the intrinsic value of one or more of the group members can be changed, for better or for worse, then moral problems can occur and principles for choosing can be formulated. Assuming that when we use the terms "more" and "less" we can speak in terms of equivalent units, we can formulate the following principles.

1. A group is better when the intrinsic good if its members is increased. This is true whether the increase is in one member, or any other member or members. That is, a group becomes better when one member obtains one more unit of intrinsic value. A group becomes better when one member obtains more units of intrinsic value even though no other members may do so. A group is better when all members obtain many more units of intrinsic good. The foregoing principle specifies nothing regarding the distribution of such goods among group members. In a group of ten members, the group as a group may be said to increase in good exactly as much when one of the members increases his good as a member by ten units while the others do not increase, as when each of the ten members increases by one unit, other things being equal. Now if there is some qualitative problem involved relative to such distribution, then things are not equal and some additional principle must be invoked. Distinction between a law of diminishing returns from added increments of instrumental goods and added increments of presumed equivalent units of intrinsic goods must be kept clear if our principle is to be understood. If an additional unit of intrinsic

good was not in fact so enjoyed, then it would not be a full additional unit, under our present premises.

The point we are making is that the "intrinsic value calculus" (i.e. the hedonistic calculus expanded to include enthusiasms, satisfactions, contentments and organically blended enjoyments) can be applied properly to the intrinsic value of a group as well as to that of an individual. Our principle, stated as a code item, is: Other things being equal, when choosing for a group and being faced with a choice between two alternatives, one of which consists in increasing and the other in not increasing the intrinsic good of members of the group, one ought always choose the former. As a subprinciple to this, one might say that, other things being equal, when choosing for a group and being faced with a choice between two alternatives, one of which consists in improving only one member of the group and the other in improving no members of the group, one ought to choose the former. (If someone should remark that increase in one without increasing the others is likely to produce envy which is experienced as an intrinsic evil, then the conditions we have specified do not prevail and the principle does not apply because not all other things are equal.)

2. A corresponding negative principle can be stated likewise. A group is worse when the intrinsic good of its members is decreased (or when the intrinsic evil of its members is increased). Hence the code item: Other things being equal, when choosing for a group and being faced with a choice between two alternatives, one of which consists in decreasing and the other in not decreasing the intrinsic good of members of the group, one ought always to choose the latter.

Group Number Variable

Principles differ when the intrinsic value of every member is considered as (a) invariable or (b) variable.

INTRINSIC VALUE PER MEMBER INVARIABLE. To the extent that the intrinsic value of each person can be considered as equal to that of every other person among the members of a group, the following principles or code items seem obvious.

1. Other things being equal, when choosing for a group and

being faced with the problem of choosing between two or more alternatives, one of which consists in adding another member whose intrinsic good is regarded as equal to that of each of the other members, and the other of which consists in not adding another member, always choose the former.

2. Other things being equal, when choosing for a group and being faced with the problem of choosing between two alternatives, one of which consists of subtracting a member whose intrinsic good is regarded as equal to that of each of the other members, and the other of which consists in not subtracting him, always choose the latter.

3. Other things being equal, when choosing for a group and being faced with the problem of choosing between two alternatives, one of which consists in adding a larger number of members, each of whose intrinsic good is regarded as equal to that of each of the present membership, and the other of which consists in adding a smaller number of such members, one ought always to choose the former.

4. Other things being equal, when choosing for a group and being faced with the problem of choosing between two alternatives, one of which consists in subtracting a larger number of members, each of whose intrinsic good is regarded as equal to that of each of the other members, and the other of which consists in subtracting a smaller number of such members, one ought always to choose the latter.

INTRINSIC VALUE PER MEMBER VARIABLE. To the extent that the intrinsic value of persons as members of a group can be considered variable, the following principles seem obvious.

1. Other things being equal, when choosing for a group and being faced with the problem of choosing between two alternatives, one of which consists in adding a person with more intrinsic good and the other of which consists in adding a person with less intrinsic good, one ought always to choose the former.

2. Other things being equal, when choosing for a group and being faced with the problem of choosing between two alternatives, one of which consists in subtracting a person with more intrinsic good and the other in subtracting a person with less intrinsic good, one ought always to choose the latter.

3. Other things being equal, when choosing for a group and being faced with the problem of choosing between two alternatives —one of which consists in adding several more persons, the average intrinsic good of which is greater than that of the present membership, and the other consists in adding the same number of persons, the average intrinsic good of which is less than that of the present membership—one ought always to choose the former.

4. Other things being equal, when choosing for a group and being faced with the problem of choosing between two alternatives —one of which consists in subtracting several persons, the average intrinsic good of which is less than the average for the remaining members of the group, and the other consists in subtracting the same number of persons, the average intrinsic good of which is greater than the average for the remaining members of the group— one ought always to choose the former.

Principles Pertaining Primarily to Instrumental Values

Many readers find themselves in more familiar territory in discussing instrumental values for, somehow, people seem much more preoccupied with means to ends than with the ends themselves. This statement appears true for both groups and individuals; we seem to be more interested in what they are *good for* than in what their ultimate goodness consists of. Here again we encounter the problem of understanding actuality and potentiality and of the "real" and "conditional" potential values discussed in Chapters 5 and 6. Fortunately, many of the problems and related principles have been studied in great detail in the science of economics. Consideration here will be limited to the most general problems and principles relative to choosing for a group.

First of all, a fundamental distinction needs to be made between (1) values of groups to individuals and (2) values of individuals to groups. Then we can also discover (3) principles pertaining to the mutual instrumentality of individuals and groups. The significance of this three-fold distinction may be strikingly illustrated by citing three historically well-known statements exemplifying principles related to each type respectively: (1) "The greatest good for the greatest number." (2) "He who does not work shall not eat."

(3) "From each according to his ability and to each according to his need." The following principles may provide a basis for reevaluating each of these statements.

Principles Pertaining to Instrumental Value of Groups to Individuals

1. Other things being equal, when choosing for a group and being faced with the problem of choosing between two alternatives, one of which consists of the greatest good which the group can produce for an individual member, and the other in less than the greatest good, one ought always to choose the former.

2. Other things being equal, when choosing for a group and being faced with the problem of choosing between two alternatives, one of which consists in the greatest good for the greatest number and the other in less than the greatest good for the greatest number, one ought always to choose the former.

Principles Pertaining to Instrumental Value of Individuals to Groups

1. Other things being equal, when choosing for a group and being faced with the problem of choosing between two alternatives, one of which consists in recommending to a member that he do the best he can for his group and the other in recommending that he do less than the best he can for his group, one ought always to choose the former.

2. Other things being equal, when choosing for a group and being faced with the problem of choosing between two alternatives, one of which consists in recommending that one member do the best he can for another member of the group and the other of which consists in recommending that he do less than the best he can for the other, one ought always to choose the former.

Principles Pertaining to the Interrelations of the Values of Members and Their Groups to Each Other

We select only one example. Other things being equal, when choosing for a group and being faced with the problem of choosing between alternatives, one of which consists both in the group doing the best it can for its members and in its members doing the best they can for it, another of which consists of a group doing the best it can for its members without their doing the best they can for it, and another of which consists of members doing the best they can for the group without the group doing its best for them, one ought always to choose the former.

The foregoing proposed principles, or code items, selected from a larger number, sufficiently illustrate surely how conditional oughts (i.e. "if all other things are equal") can be stated as universal principles with precision or exactitude. We have not here exemplified nonuniversal principles based on statistical probabilities resulting from empirical evidence which also play important roles in ethics as a behavioral science. Many such principles have already been experimentally demonstrated within other specialized sciences, such as economics, physiology and physics. The interdependence of ethics and other behavioral sciences, and of behavioral sciences and all other sciences, is too often overlooked by ethicists. For every principle about uniformities in existing processes which may function as a factor in making actual decisions may thereby serve as a basis for a conditional ought, so all principles demonstrated by all sciences which may serve in this way also constitute a part of the stock of principles available to ethics as a science.

INDEX

201